The **BIG** Book
of Business Games

John Newstrom and Ed Scannell are authors of the best-selling McGraw-Hill series, *Games Trainers Play,* including:

GAMES TRAINERS PLAY

MORE GAMES TRAINERS PLAY

STILL MORE GAMES TRAINERS PLAY

EVEN MORE GAMES TRAINERS PLAY

THE COMPLETE GAMES TRAINERS PLAY

The BIG Book of Business Games

Icebreakers, Creativity Exercises, and Meeting Energizers

John W. Newstrom

Edward E. Scannell

McGraw-Hill

New York   San Francisco   Washington, D.C.   Auckland   Bogotá
Caracas   Lisbon   London   Madrid   Mexico City   Milan
Montreal   New Delhi   San Juan   Singapore
Sydney   Tokyo   Toronto

Library of Congress Cataloging-in-Publication Data

Newstrom, John W.
    The big book of business games : icebreakers, creativity
exercises, and meeting energizers. / John Newstrom and Edward E.
Scannell.
        p.   cm.
    ISBN 0-07-046476-6
    1. Management games.   2. Communication in management.   3. Business
meetings.   4. Decision-making.   I. Scannell, Edward E.   II. Title.
HD30.26.N49   1995
658.4'0353—dc20   95-44899
                                                                                      CIP

McGraw-Hill

*A Division of The **McGraw-Hill** Companies*

4 5 6 7 8 9 10   FGRFGR   9 9 8

ISBN 0-07-046476-6

*The sponsoring editor for this book was Richard Narramore, the editing su-
pervisor was Fred Dahl, and the production supervisor was Donald F.
Schmidt. It was set in Frugal Sans by Inkwell Publishing Services.*

Contents

Acknowledgments

Any project like this is always a team effort. There is no way we could possibly thank the thousands of "team members" who have continually encouraged and assisted us in our continuing quest to make meetings more effective.

To the thousands of friends and colleagues who have attended our seminars and workshops for such groups as the American Society for Training and Development, Meeting Professionals, Int'l., and the National Speakers Association, we are most grateful. They have helped us field-test the items in this book and have contributed to many of its ideas.

For the continuining assistance from the McGraw-Hill team of Philip Ruppel and Richard Narramore, we are truly indebted. They have become friends as well as our publishing team.

Most importantly, a very special thanks to Sue Hershkowitz-Scannell and Diane Newstrom, who have given us the love, patience, understanding, and encouragement that have truly helped us grow both personally and professionally.

Thank you!

The **BIG** Book
of Business Games

Introduction to Business Games

Games? Games for *businesspeople*? You've got to be kidding!

Believe us—we're not kidding at all. As a matter of fact, we're quite serious about this business, and we're in total agreement that the world of "business" is serious business indeed. So whether you're the boss, the sales manager, the team leader, or anyone else who occasionally has the responsibility of conducting meetings or giving a presentation, then this book is clearly for you!

Conducting Board, Staff, Team, and Committee Meetings

How do you keep the board meeting from becoming a "bored" meeting? The same question, of course, could be posed for staff, sales, or committee meetings, or, for that matter, for just about any kind of group get-together. How's *your* team functioning? Could meetings with your team members be more productive?

Ask almost any colleague about meetings, and you'll likely get a response clearly less than positive. In fact, many of us would emphatically state that far too many meetings are a waste of time. Unfortunately, in many organizations, they are!

Many meetings miss their mark simply for the lack of planning or preparation. One study of over 1000 middle managers identified the top three reasons why meetings fail:

1. Getting off the subject
2. Lack of agenda or goals
3. Lasting too long

Sound familiar? How about the meeting you ran the other day? How much time and money are wasted every day in meetings that are unproductive? Every business day, wasteful meetings are held—far too often with the same negative results. Games, however, can make your meetings more engaging, more productive, and more cost-effective.

Using Games in Meetings

Games have been used to supplement and upgrade meetings ever since it was discovered that people have very short attention spans! In fact, studies claim that the span of attention for most of us varies anywhere from ten seconds to three or four minutes! It's easy to see, then, why people become easily bored (or overwhelmed) with technical material and respond much better when a meeting has life and variety. In addition, our television-oriented society has conditioned many of us to expect drama, excitement, and involvement in our everyday lives. In short, group members, especially those of Generation X, expect meetings to be lively, fast-paced, innovative, participative, and imaginative. (Just for the fun of it, how many of those words describe your last meeting?) Games can materially help accomplish these objectives by focusing attention on the needs of the attendees, not on those of the meeting leader.

Characteristics of Games

The unique features of games make them usable and appropriate for a number of your meetings. Games usually:

1. *Are quick to use.* They can range from a five- or ten-second physical activity, through a one-minute visual illustration or verbal vignette, up to a 20- or 30-minute group discussion exercise. However, since the activity should be used to add to or supplement the main purpose or content of the meeting, the time devoted to the game should be minimal.

2. *Are inexpensive.* In general, nothing has to be purchased, nor does an outside facilitator or consultant have to be engaged. With few exceptions, the games included in this book can be used at little, if any, cost.

3. *Are participative.* To be used effectively, the games should involve the participants physically (through movement) or psychologically (through visual or mental activity, thought, or action). Games typically help people focus their attention, and make them think, react, speak, and, most importantly, have fun while doing their jobs!

4. *Use props.* Several of the games involve the use of a single prop or outside material to add realism to the activity. These props could be as simple as a picture, a person, or an inanimate object.

5. *Are low-risk.* All the games in this book have been field-tested dozens of times in a variety of meetings with a variety of different groups. When matched to the proper content, the right context, the right people, and the right climate, and when used in a positive manner, they will always work for you. The games are user-friendly, and people respond to them positively.

6. *Are adaptable.* The best activities, like the best humorous stories, can be adapted to fit almost any situation, and reinforce the points you want to make in your meeting. They can be modified slightly and still retain their original flavor and character. In fact, it is highly recommended that you tailor the game as much as possible to fit your goals.

7. *Are single-focus.* Games are best used when they demonstrate or illustrate just one major point. As such, they are oriented to micro issues rather than macro issues. Keep them simple and focused, and they will do their job for you!

Adult Learning

"What," you might ask, "does adult learning have to do with the way I run my meetings?" As a matter of fact, it has *everything* to do with the way you run meetings! If you doubt that for a moment, think of the last time you sat in on a meeting where someone "lectured" to you, or insulted your intelligence, or seemed to be oblivious to the fact they were talking to adults and not a class of first-graders.

With that in mind, here are a few ideas about adult learning that will help you for your next meeting. Doubtless, hundreds of studies have investigated how the learning process takes place. Of the many resulting theories and principles, a few seem to have the most direct implications—and applications—for use in conducting meetings.

Learning and why games are good learning experiences

First, what do we mean by "learning"? We're referring here to knowledge that is obtained by study. Learning is the act of acquiring knowledge, skills, or attitudes. It's also been defined as self-development through self-activity. Most authorities on the learning process agree that learning is a lifelong process. For our purpose, we'll state that learning is a change in behavior as the result of an experience. In brief, learning means change!

A few of the more commonly accepted principles that are most relevant to energizing a staff meeting or a sleepy audience can be converted to "laws of learning":

1. Law of Effect
2. Law of Exercise
3. Law of Readiness
4. Law of Association

As you look at these four principles, you will quickly learn why the use of games and other activities clearly ties in with these theories. Moreover, because games always involve the group, they are usually well accepted.

1. *Law of Effect:* Essentially, people learn best in pleasant surroundings. They tend to accept and repeat activities that are both pleasant and satisfying to them. The importance of climate-setting activities, for example, is underscored when we realize how we all tend to make first impressions very quickly. Think back to a time when you were new to a group and didn't know anyone else in the room. Or when you went to a meeting and everyone seemed to know everybody else—except you! If you're like most of us, you were probably uncomfortable. How about that new person on your team or the new hire in your department? How do you suppose he or she feels the first few days on the job? Obviously, these same feelings persist.

The Law of Effect tells us that we can overcome those fears and anxieties by a climate-setting activity or game. By making people feel a part of the group, as opposed to apart *from* the group, we establish a warm, hospitable atmosphere, as well as a comfortable working environment.

2. *Law of Exercise:* Practice makes perfect! Although we've heard this statement hundreds of times, it may not be true! Mere talking is not the best way to convince a group of your point. If you want to make an important point with a group, a game can be the way to do it! More to the point, we are safe in saying that "People learn by doing." It is a proven fact that people remember something much better if it is tied to some kind of active, physical involvement. Since games and activities invariably have built-in participation, they vividly demonstrate the importance of repetition for learning.

3. *Law of Readiness:* This principle relates to motivation and the internal desire people have to do a good job. For example, you might have the best speech, the best agenda, or the best hi-tech visual aids available. But if the person on the receiving end is not ready, willing, or able to learn, your best efforts as coach or communicator will prove futile. Often, this law also has relevance to the time of day, day of week, etc. For example, most people tend to get a bit sleepy right after the lunch hour. If you're holding a staff, sales, or departmental meeting at 1 P.M., you know you're going to see some sleepy people! Because games are so participant-oriented and are often fun to play, motivation is enhanced.

4. *Law of Association:* This is the basis for much of our learning, both as adults as well as children. If we can bring new information that builds on knowledge already garnered, this new material is that much more easily assimilated.

Picture, for example, a toddler playing with building blocks on the floor. How the child carefully places one block atop another is similar to the way we "put things together" in the adult world. We go from one thing to another (one block atop another). We go from the "known" to the "unknown" in an easy, methodical fashion. Each new "block" of information or knowledge is added to our existing storehouse of knowledge, skills, or attitudes. When used properly, the experiential learning techniques used in games emphasize this law by illustrating what the game intended to show or teach. Thus, in a seemingly obscure but enjoyable way, we've added to that person's knowledge base.

Obviously, these four principles are not intended to be an exhaustive listing of the dozens of other theories or rules we have experienced. They do, however, seem to capture the most important and pragmatic basics of why games are such useful communication tools. Unfortunately, as simple and practical as these few principles are, we continually see violations of them in meetings, in programs, and in a host of other activities. Anyone can learn these rules. The astute businessperson not only knows these applications, but, more importantly, incorporates them every day in leading meetings and working in group settings.

Summary

Although it might seem that games are designed just to have fun, in reality most games can communicate a point more effectively than just talking. Games are misused if they are used simply to "kill time" or inflate one's ego. Remember that games are always the adjunct or supplement to a meeting, and therefore should not be the main focus of it. We know that learning can be fun; why shouldn't meetings and other presentations be fun too?

How to Use This Book

The Simplicity of Games

Games are a fun way to support the objectives of a meeting or presentation. As discussed in Chap. 1, games are typically very brief, easy-to-use, inexpensive, highly involving, field-tested, and virtually certain to produce a meaningful outcome. In fact, many of them provide an "Aha!" experience whether or not the participants "succeed" in the game's task, because the focus is often on the process used, not on the outcome.

Here's a classic activity, originally used by Allen Solem at the University of Minnesota. Called "Remodeling a Window," it is designed to show group members how rigid perceptions of situations can cause communication breakdowns.

Directions: Tell group members a story about how you purchased a house, but found to your dismay that one room had only a small window and was therefore quite dark. Upon measuring the window, you noted that it was 2 feet wide and 2 feet high. When pressed by your spouse to brighten the room, you agreed to do so. You took your saw and cut out some of the wall surrounding the window and inserted a new, larger window that clearly let in more light (twice as much as previously). When your spouse remeasured the new window, however, you both noted with surprise that the measurements (2 feet by 2 feet) were precisely the same as before. It seems almost impossible—more light is now coming through a space that measures the same height and width as before! How can this be so?

Ask the group for explanations, eventually focusing the group's attention on the definition and use of the word "window." Inquire about the perceived shape of a typical window (perhaps have them draw a picture on a sheet of paper). Most drawings will be square or rectangular. Then draw a picture of your particular window, which was diamond-shaped (see Fig. 2-1a). By superim-

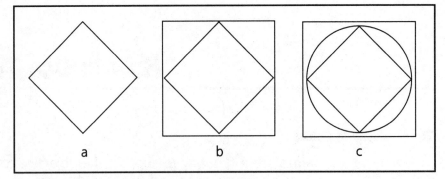

Figure 2-1 Different perceptions of window shapes.

posing a second drawing of a square with the same vertical and horizontal dimensions (Fig. 2-1b) or even a circle with a diameter of 2 feet (Fig. 2-1c), you can demonstrate the feasibility of "enlarging" the window without changing the basic dimensions of it. The key lies in one's *perception of the problem* (one's image of a window). Point out that many common words have multiple meanings, which can lead to confusion and misinterpretation not only by members of one's own culture, but especially by members of different cultures. Members can then be invited to brainstorm action plans for prevention or reduction of such problems.

This example illustrates one of the best uses of business games—to provide a vivid image that implants in recipients' minds the major message or theme of the moment. Used in this way, games increase the likelihood of retention while drawing on participants' intellect and creative abilities in a temporary departure from a more serious presentation of material. In short, games help people to have *fun* while *learning a key point.*

Selecting an Appropriate Game

The games in this book are classified by their purpose or teaching objective:

- *Climate setting.* Good presenters catch and hold the group's attention at the beginning of each working session. Games are useful devices to "warm up" a group, break the ice among strangers, and focus participants' thoughts on the task at hand. In addition, games can be used to add a bit of energy to the end of a long session or to stimulate the group to action. Several of the games are designed to facilitate transfer of learning from the meeting back to the work environment.

- *Motivating.* What motivates people to contribute extra effort, to "go the extra mile"? What role do financial incentives play? How much of an influence is competition? How important is positive reinforcement? Although motivation is often taken for granted, some simple but vivid lessons can be learned, and the games in this section are among the most powerful ones available for inducing members to confront their own and others' needs.

- *Stimulating problem solving.* How can you get group members to break out of their old paradigms? How can you get them to look for problems and attack them in new ways? These are challenging tasks, and they won't be solved in a single session. Nevertheless, it is important that group members accept the importance of being creative, recognizing their own limitations, and searching for new ways to solve existing problems. Some games provide useful avenues by which to approach these issues.

- *Managing change.* Writers James Belasco and Rosabeth Moss Kanter have both referred, in their best-selling books, to the challenges inherent in getting large organizations (which they characterized as "elephants" or "giants") to change. Yet Tom Peters, Peter Vaill, and Peter Senge all argue persuasively that these are turbulent, chaotic, "white-water" times requiring the anticipation of problems and development of flexible responses. How can you get group members to accept the need for change, and begin to act on that need? Games can be useful starting points for this purpose.

- *Surfacing hidden problems.* What can you do when it becomes apparent that there are problems that no one wishes to talk about (undiscussables)? According to noted author Chris Argyris, people engage in defensive reasoning in their efforts to protect themselves, and they eventually sink to the level of skilled incompetence. Your task is to create a climate of openness and constructive confrontation, and games can provide a useful vehicle for stimulating this behavior in a "safe" environment.

- *Team building.* Why are some groups cohesive and others not? Why do some seem to be instantly productive, while others move only slowly in that direction? How can you encourage group members to look at themselves, and see the need for a change from individualism to collective effort? The games in this section are useful stimulants for legitimizing candid conversation about what it means to be a team, and starting an inventory of a team's strengths and resources.

- *Presentation boosters.* Every employee, at some time, is called on to give a formal or semiformal presentation. Sometimes the presentational skills used on those occasions can make or break the project, despite the idea's intrinsic merits. How do you get and hold a group's attention? How can you inject enthusiasm into your audience? What are some creative ways to introduce yourself or another to a group? Games can provide useful tools to address these issues.

- *Improving communications.* How important are listening skills in your group, and are they being practiced effectively? Are group members open- or closed-minded? Do members pay attention to nonverbal cues when they are available? Does communication ever get distorted because of the assumptions members make or their failure to follow directions? You may believe that your group members aren't as effective as you would like them to be, and therefore find the games in this section especially appropriate for identifying problems and relevant solutions.

Preparing Game Materials

It is valuable to look ahead and anticipate which games may be appropriate for a given meeting. After selecting one or more games, you can often save much time by preparing the appropriate handout, transparency, or flip chart in advance.

Introducing a Game

In general, a brief explanation and background for a game should be given. It is important to *provide a context for the activity*—a framework to help the group members see where it fits into the meeting's agenda. Get their undivided attention, solicit their co-operation, share appropriate information, assign them their task, and clearly specify the time limits. It is imperative that the inter-action be monitored and that group discussion be ended on schedule.

Leading a Group Discussion

Games will remain just games in the absence of effective facili-tated discussion. Look over the entire set of materials provided. Anticipate probable results and reactions. Prepare not only the questions provided, but also additional ones that allow you to tai-lor the results to your own organization. Indicate the time limits available for discussing the game. Focus intensively on the mean-ing and purpose of a game, while minimizing conversation on the mechanics of the game itself. Make the participants responsible for generating meaningful conclusions; don't be too quick to in-sert your own opinions and observations. Keep the discussion flowing rapidly, and terminate it when all major points have been brought to light.

Making the Transition to Applications

All of the games provided here are generic, meaning that they are broad in nature and not restricted to any one organization or industry. It is imperative that you shift the group's attention from a focus on *what* happened in the game to clear attention on what it *means* and what its *significance* is. Encourage par-ticipants to consider questions like "What will I remember from the game tomorrow? What does it illustrate? How can I use it?" Then make a record of the key learning points raised and the action plans developed, and distribute it to the group for later reference.

General Guidelines for Using Games

After more than two decades of experience with games for various types of businesspersons, we have learned a number of important lessons (see Fig. 2-2). Although the guidelines we present here appear to be incredibly simple, they are vitally important to your success. We urge you to study these five generic rules carefully and follow them closely.

1. *Select games carefully.* This requires early immersion in the entire set of games for each identified objective so as to develop reasonable familiarity with the nature and requirements of each before choosing one or more for use with your group. Before making a final selection, consider whether the particular game fits your presentational style, the objectives for the group meeting, and the participants themselves.

2. *Consult with others.* Talk with other users of games, and tap into their experiences with various activities. For example, you might inquire of them:

   Have you used this game?

   What happened?

   Would you use it again?

   What would you change next time?

   Do you know a good alternative?

   Where can I find it?

   Create your own (possibly in-house) network of game users that you can draw on for support.

3. *Have an objective.* Some persons jump into using a game but lack a well thought-out, clearly articulated idea of what they hope to accomplish with it. They lack an objective—the logical starting point. As a result, many of them use a game only (and inappropriately) because it was available, handy, or looked interesting. You must do a high-quality job of selecting games that fit your objectives, and then communicate that purpose to the group members.

4. *Have a back-up plan.* If you believe in Murphy's law ("What can go wrong, probably will!"), it would be wise to have more than one game available, similar to having a "Plan B." A prop may break, the group may have "played" that particular game just last week while you were on vacation, or they may prove to be unresponsive to a certain type of game. Be ready with an alternative.

5. *Pretest the game.* A skeptic once advised people to trust no one's promises except those from God, and "even then make sure that you get it in writing!" Heeding this ultraconservative advice, game users should not rely totally on the description provided with the game, or on someone else's recommendation of it as a sure-fire winner. Find a safe context in which to experiment with it before gambling your reputation on it. Close colleagues, volunteer staff, or family members are remarkably good critics. Use them.

Tips for Using Games in Meetings

In addition to the general guidelines just provided, we offer you five additional rules applicable to the use of games in small group meetings, and five others that apply more specifically to formal and informal presentations. For example, in your first group meeting, you may wish to try the classic "dollar exchange/idea exchange" exercise, which goes like this:

Directions: Ask for the loan of a dollar from a member of the group. Display it prominently in one hand, and proceed to ask for the loan of a second dollar from another person. Then carefully repay the first loaner with the second dollar and repay the second loaner with the first dollar. Now ask the rhetorical question, "Is either of these persons now richer than they were before?" (Neither, of course, is.) Then point out to the group that by contrast had two ideas been shared as readily, not only the respective givers, but *all* participants would be richer in experience than they were previously.

Now inquire: What factors *discourage* us from sharing useful ideas and insights with others? How can we overcome or diminish these? What factors *encourage* us to share ideas with other group members? How can we increase these?

General Rules:

1. Select them carefully.
2. Consult with others.
3. Have an objective.
4. Have a back-up plan.
5. Pretest the game.

Tips for Group Meetings:

1. Choose low-risk activities.
2. Be brief and selective.
3. Be creative.
4. Evaluate your use of games.
5. Lighten up.

Tips for Presentations:

1. Don't use games just to entertain.
2. Be prepared.
3. Know the answer.
4. Anticipate some resistance.
5. Anticipate recall of the game, not the message.

Figure 2-2 Business game guidelines.

As you can see by this example, games for meetings can be incredibly simple. Nevertheless, with regard to meetings, we urge you to:

1. *Choose low-risk activities.* You should always take care not to offend your group members. Do not place them at unnecessary levels of physical or psychological risk. Never purposely antagonize the group members. Always screen the games so that you can feel comfortable knowing it is a "can't miss" experience.

2. *Be brief and selective.* Time is a vital resource, and organizations can't afford to waste it. The majority of the games presented here can be introduced and used in relatively short

time periods. However, tips are also provided indicating how to expand on the discussion if that proves desirable. Always remember that the game is *not* the major part of the group session. It is only an aid to achieve your other results and goals. Don't drag the game out, and don't use too many within a single session. Think of games as an appetizer or dessert, but not as the main course of a meal. Games are a means to a serious end, but not an end in themselves.

3. *Be creative.* Just as doctors warn us of hardening of the arteries, game users need to be warned of "hardening of the categories." Search for ways to *adapt* or tailor a game to best fit your purpose for the particular group at hand. Always be on the lookout for new ways to make your point within a meeting. Stay flexible.

4. *Evaluate your use of games.* Keep close tabs on the frequency of use with a group, the game's apparent impact on the group's learning and retention, and the group's reaction to or reception of your games. It is all too easy to fall into ruts, such as using the same games again and again in subsequent meetings, or even overusing games and exercises to the detriment of the intended message. Audit yourself on your use of games, and resolve to update and expand your repertoire of games by periodically replacing the weaker ones.

5. *Lighten up.* Keeping in mind all the preceding caveats and guidelines explained, take your task seriously—but don't take yourself too seriously. Group members will be even more on your side when they detect that you are a "real" person— someone who can laugh at yourself and allow minor deviations from a structured exercise. Above all, have fun, and make it fun for the group!

Tips for Using Games in Presentations

Games can be exceptionally useful devices for catching and holding the audience's attention during large group presentations. Sometimes they are as simple as the following technique suggests.

Directions: Ask the audience members to name the single thing that each person is most afraid of. (They may mention snakes, spiders, falling, closed spaces, tornados, etc.) Then disclose to them that, according to David Wallechinsky in *The Book of Lists,* "speaking before a group" is the worst human fear in the United States.

Now ask them to identify all the things a person could do to help overcome the fear of speaking in front of an audience. The list will likely be long, including such items as preparing your material well, practicing repeatedly, using involvement, establishing your credibility, anticipating problems, using members' names, establishing eye contact, practicing responses to tough questions, anticipating major problems, dressing comfortably, getting there early, taking a deep breath before you begin, etc.

Now summarize what has taken place: By preparing properly, you have diminished your fear of speaking by involving them (which takes the pressure off you). At the same time you've evoked from them a highly practical list of suggestions from which the entire audience can benefit!

Nevertheless, we offer these restrictive guidelines for helping you to be more effective in presentational situations.

1. *Don't use games just to entertain.* While it is true that many games contain an element of "fun," don't get caught in the trap of being seen as using too much gimmickry in your presentations. By overrelying on only the "fun stuff," you mark yourself as more of an entertainer rather than as a person who emphasizes substance for instructive ends. Today's workforce is too serious and sophisticated to be treated lightly; don't waste valuable presentation time by using a game solely to entertain.

2. *Be prepared.* An old adage suggests that the three most important parts of any presentation are (1) preparation, (2) preparation, and (3) preparation. After deciding to use a game, prepare for it thoroughly; never select one at the last minute. Make certain that you are totally familiar with it, that your goals are clearly defined, and that you have a definite plan for debriefing the audience at the game's conclusion so as to clearly illustrate the related points.

3. *Know the answer* (if one exists). Early in his career, one of this book's authors wound up with the proverbial "egg on his face" when audience members requested the answer to a game and he discovered that he could not immediately respond off the top of his head. The lesson that day for us was the value of preparing a visual "key" that could be pulled out if our minds should again go blank under pressure. And that bit of preparation is always a wise practice when preparing for a presentation!

4. *Anticipate some resistance.* You may occasionally encounter audience members who believe that games are "silly." Although we believe it is best for learning when everyone is actively involved, one option is to call for a group of volunteers and let the rest of the audience act as observers. Another option is to provide a clear explanation of the purpose of the activity, enlist the group's help in making it work, and promise them that the meaning will become clear during the debriefing.

5. *Anticipate recall of the game, not the message.* Several years ago one of the authors led a one-week workshop and used a number of games, all of which seemed to fulfill their objectives. Toward the end of the week, one of the participants asked if she could give a short summary of the week's activities on the last day. The author eagerly agreed, and looked forward to the report with great anticipation. However, the report presented was a (facetious) litany of the highlights of all the *games* that had been used, rather than the expected summary of the essential *content.* After a good laugh, the author used the occasion to turn the group's attention once more to the key learning points, where the emphasis needed to be placed.

Danger Zones in Using Games

We *want* you to succeed in your use of games. Therefore, we need to provide a balanced perspective on games by identifying some of the disadvantages and pitfalls to offset the enthusiasm that we have been exhibiting throughout Chaps. 1 and 2. Figure 2-3 identifies a series of potential difficulties or limitations, many

1. Props needed
2. Time requirements
3. Preparation
4. Simplistic image
5. Inappropriate usage
6. Distraction from learning
7. Overly complicated
8. Personally threatening

Figure 2-3 Danger zones in the use of games.

of which can be minimized through careful planning and adequate preparation.

1. *Props.* Some games require the use of certain props, which are usually simple and conveniently available. A few, however, may prove to be inconvenient to obtain or assemble on short notice, especially without adequate lead time before the session in which they will be used.

2. *Time.* A few games or expanded versions of existing games can require more time than you are willing to devote. It is incumbent on you to chart the process, tightly structure the discussion, and know when to call a halt.

3. *Preparation.* Games vary in the depth of background required to conduct them properly. Some require no special preparation, while others may be enriched by one's unique educational background, in-depth reading, or expertise in group processing skills (i.e., drawing out the major points illustrated in the game by means of a spirited group discussion).

4. *Image.* Some games may be perceived as overly simplistic and sophomoric in nature, by some participants, while being relevant and vivid to others. You need to gauge the sophistication of your group in relation to the game to be used, and perhaps pretest the proposed game on one or two participants.

In addition to the preceding structural limitations, there are also some pitfalls in your use of games. It is possible that insecure, inexperienced, or unprepared individuals may use a game to kill time, to impress colleagues with how smart they are, or even to "put down" group members by setting them up to fail on a game. Any time that playing games begins to dominate the focus of a group's interactive process, they should be used with less regularity. They are designed to be *supportive tools,* not the purpose of group meetings. Similarly, if most participants perceive that the games are "hokey" or cute, but are simultaneously distracting from the overall goal of the session, more careful explanation and judicious use are in order. You should always encourage participants to demand (and contribute) answers to the questions of "So what?" or "What's in it for me?" for each game, and there should always be one (or preferably more) substantive answers. Finally, good games should not become overly complicated, nor should they in any way be allowed to become personally threatening or demeaning to a participant.

Key Points to Remember

1. Sharpen your professional group-facilitation skills by seeking and obtaining a balance between your emphasis on technical content (being issue-focused) and group process (how things are taking place). Seek to become a "balanced contributor."

2. Games are invaluable aids that can contribute not only to higher participant satisfaction with meetings, but also to the creation of learning individuals and a learning organization. This is a higher goal worth striving for.

3. Games can help to "warm up" a group or team before it gets underway on its work agenda. Games can legitimize the involvement of all participants, introduce and illustrate a point vividly, or close a group session with high impact.

4. A broad array of games should be reviewed before selecting the most feasible one(s). Then they should be pretested and matched against the specific objectives for that group meeting. Outcomes should be anticipated, alternatives prepared, limitations recognized, and some plan for assessment of their success should be implemented.

Summary

Games can contribute to both the content and process objectives of a group meeting. Most importantly, they facilitate member learning, retention, and application, while also making the meeting itself more enjoyable. Games can be used:

- As icebreakers.
- To illustrate key points.
- To involve participants.
- To stimulate the recognition of the need for change.
- To surface hidden problems.
- To close a working session with high impact.

Numerous guidelines have been presented to increase the likelihood of your first-time success. These guidelines are directed toward the selection, use, and evaluation of games, and are drawn from the experience of hundreds of applications. Above all, you are urged to keep games in their proper perspective, recognizing that most are designed to facilitate the acquisition, retention, or application of a change in learning by participants—and to interject a bit of fun in the process. Only if they are legitimately providing this function should these games be used.

1

Climate Setting, Icebreakers, and Session Openers

EASY WAYS TO BREAK THE ICE

OBJECTIVE

To provide a variety of quick options for "warming up" a group of strangers, or workmates who may not interact socially

MATERIALS

Extra name tags; felt-tipped markers; Nerf ball

PROCEDURE

- ✓ Ask each group member to think of a nickname—one that they have had, now have, or would like to have.
- ✓ Have them write it on an index card and a stick-on name tag.
- ✓ Ask them to turn the name tag face down temporarily.
- ✓ Then collect the index cards.
- ✓ Now read the cards one at a time, asking the group to guess who "belongs" to each nickname.
- ✓ As the group identifies each person, ask that each individual wear the appropriate name tag for the remainder of the meeting.

DISCUSSION QUESTIONS

1. What do you each feel about disclosing "personal" information about yourself at work? What are the potential gains, and possible risks?
2. What possible "norms" for future meetings does this suggest to us?
3. What other questions should we pose in future group sessions?

TIPS

- ✓ Control the amount of time tightly (and announce this in advance), or some individuals may get carried away on the details of their explanation.

✓ Carefully gauge your group to determine the appropriate type of question to ask. Don't ask a group of likely low risk-takers to disclose their greatest hidden fears or worst failures in life—at least not the first time you try this!

✓ It is tempting to allow a group member to respond (e.g., "Oh, I didn't know that you like Madonna's music! Let me tell you about the concert of hers I once attended ..."). Instead, urge them to wait until a refreshment break or luncheon conversation to "connect" further with the other person.

IF YOU HAVE MORE TIME

Prior to the session, survey the group members to discover various information such as their hobbies, major nonwork accomplishments, pet peeves, self-descriptive adjectives, etc. Then prepare a brief synopsis of each person (with name deleted) and distribute the summaries to the group at the beginning of the session. Encourage them to be observant and attentive to any clues provided during the meeting. During the last few minutes, return to the list and ask them to identify the person that they think is described by each synopsis (and why they now think so).

Alternatively, ask the members to sit or stand in a circle. Throw a soft (sponge-like) ball to one person and ask that individual to tell their name and disclose something about themselves—an unusual event that happened in their lives, a special talent they have, their dream vacation, or the living person they most admire (and why). Then ask them to throw the ball to another person who has not yet received it, and repeat the process. Continue this until all members have introduced themselves.

WHO ARE YOU?

OBJECTIVE

To enable participants to become acquainted with others in an informal setting

MATERIALS

Paper, pens or pencils

PROCEDURE

✓ Ask the individuals in your team or work group to jot down three questions they would like to ask a person they are about to meet. Suggest that they be a little creative and stay away from the more obvious inquiries, i.e., name, position, etc.

✓ After allowing one or two minutes to think up some questions, ask the group to start moving around, exchanging questions and answers with others in the room. Encourage the group to meet as many new people as possible.

✓ After five or ten minutes, reassemble the group and have each person stand and simply say their name. As each person does this, ask others to shout out something they just learned about the person standing. Allow for three or four additional items for each person before moving on to the next person.

DISCUSSION QUESTIONS

1. What were some of the more interesting things you discovered?
2. Did anyone find some things in common with others?
3. What was the most interesting question you were posed?
4. What was the funniest response you received?

TIPS

✓ Keep the introductions moving quickly.

✓ If someone stands and no one else remembers anything about that person, quickly ask that person to state two or three things from their own questions.

BINGO GAME

OBJECTIVE

To be used as a get-acquainted activity in large groups

MATERIALS

Copies of the Bingo Card, pens or pencils

PROCEDURE

✓ Tell the group it's time to play Bingo. Distribute a copy of the bingo card to each person.

✓ Each person must get up, move around the room, and find someone who fits a particular blank on the card. That person signs or initials that particular slot. For example, if Ken Brown drives a pickup, he would write his name in the appropriate space on your card.

Note: No one can sign another's card in more than one blank, even though they may qualify for more than one category.

TIPS

✓ Tell the group they can be as creative as they want in locating certain prospects. (For example, in trying to locate someone to fill in their last spot, standing on a chair calling "who's got grandkids!")

✓ Depending on the size of the group or the time available, use either an abbreviated Bingo (i.e., four corners, diagonals, etc.) or the entire card.

✓ If the members of the group know one another already, tailor the card in advance by finding out little-known facts about each person. For example, in an earlier conversation or phone call with Sue, you learned she was a high school cheerleader, etc. Either mix or match these items with the generic listing as shown, or construct a special card with these individual items for the group involved.

BINGO GAME

Directions: Each blank space identifies something about the people in this
_____ (seminar, meeting, session, etc.). Seek out your fellow participants and, if one of the listed items pertains to someone, have that person sign his or her name in the appropriate place on your Bingo card. (Even though more than one item may be relevant to a person, that individual may sign only one blank spot.)

PLAYS TENNIS	IS WEARING RED	PLAYS SOCCER	LIKES CATS	HAS GRAND-CHILDREN
_____	_____	_____	_____	_____
DRIVES A SPORTS CAR	HATES FOOTBALL	LOVES FOOTBALL	FLIES A PLANE	SPEAKS FOREIGN LANGUAGE
_____	_____	_____	_____	_____
PLAYS PIANO	HAS TROPICAL FISH	FREE	SKIS	BUYS LOTTERY TICKETS
_____	_____	_____	_____	_____
HAS RED HAIR	HATES SPINACH	HAS TWO CHILDREN	LIKES CAMPING	HAS ATTENDED OLYMPICS
_____	_____	_____	_____	_____
SINGLE PARENT	DRIVES PICKUP	BROWN EYES	READS *NEWSWEEK*	VISITED FOREIGN COUNTRY
_____	_____	_____	_____	_____

THE 30-SECOND MONOLOG

OBJECTIVE

To allow attendees at small group meetings, meal functions, and other occasions to become quickly acquainted

MATERIALS

None

PROCEDURE

This activity is designed to be used at the start of weekly or monthly organization luncheon or dinner meetings, as well as at internal departmental or staff meetings.

✓ After all participants are seated at their respective tables, announce it is time for the 30-Second Monolog. Each person will be given 30 seconds to tell those at their table anything about themselves, e.g., job position, organization, how long with the company, family, hobbies, and so on.

✓ The program chairperson calls time after the first 30 seconds, and then the second person (in clockwise fashion) has 30 seconds for his/her introduction. Continue at 30-second intervals for three to five minutes, or until each person has had the chance to make a self-introduction. (Note: Each table handles only those seated at that table, i.e., they don't speak to the entire room.)

✓ For internal staff meetings where individuals know each other, make the assignment more avocational (i.e., family, hobbies, last weekend's activities, and the like).

TIPS

✓ Before you introduce the exercise, give an example by telling the group a bit about yourself. If possible, inject humor.

✓ Since noise may be a factor, have a bell, whistle, or chime to call time after each 30-second interval.

TREASURE HUNT

OBJECTIVE

To allow new hires, new staff or team members, or members of any such group who have not previously worked together to get acquainted

MATERIALS

A copy of the Treasure Hunt handout for each person, pens or pencils

PROCEDURE

✓ At the beginning of the meeting, explain the importance of teamwork, camaraderie, etc., as well as the importance of becoming acquainted with their new team or friends.

✓ Hand out a copy of Treasure Hunt to each person.

✓ Ask that everyone find another person with at least one similarity (e.g., "grew up in Phoenix"), and one dissimilar trait (e.g., "sports fan" vs. "dislike sports"). Complete this process for at least eight to ten other participants in the meeting. (Time usually does not permit everyone participating.)

✓ Award nominal prizes to the first few people completing the form.

DISCUSSION QUESTIONS

1. How many of us tend to be reticent on first meeting new friends?

2. Did you find this exercise "nonthreatening"?

3. Did some of you find some strange things in common?

TIPS

To get the activity going, consider "walking through" one or two similar and dissimilar traits for one or two people.

TREASURE HUNT

Directions: Circulate around the room, finding one trait you have in common (such as "newcomer to city") and one item dissimilar ("has worked for same organization over 10 years" vs. "third job this year!" for example) for each of the first 10 people you meet. Note their names.

	Name	*Alike*	*Different*
1.	_____	_____	_____
2.	_____	_____	_____
3.	_____	_____	_____
4.	_____	_____	_____
5.	_____	_____	_____
6.	_____	_____	_____
7.	_____	_____	_____
8.	_____	_____	_____
9.	_____	_____	_____
10.	_____	_____	_____

LIMERICKS

OBJECTIVE

To serve as an entertaining method of getting acquainted in a social or business setting

MATERIALS

3 × 5 index cards

PROCEDURE

✓ Gather a number of limericks or well-known poems that consist of only five lines.

✓ Write one line of each limerick or poem on an index card. Do this for the first four lines, but not for the fifth.

✓ Randomly, hand out a card to each person.

✓ Ask group members to move around the room and find the three people who have the other three lines to that respective limerick.

✓ When the team is formed, tell them that their job is to create a fifth line to their limerick, other than the well-known one, and to create an activity to illustrate their poem.

TIPS

✓ Collect limericks that are readily identifiable and would be well-known by most participants.

✓ Tell the group that this exercise is strictly "for fun" and to "lighten up" in their creativity.

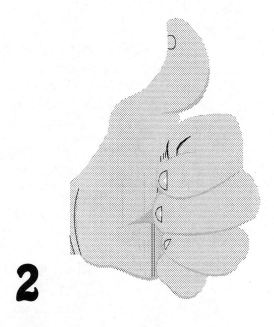

2

Motivating Your Group

WARM FUZZIES FEEL SOOOOOOO GOOD!

OBJECTIVE

To stimulate individuals to recognize, and satisfy, others' needs for positive feedback

MATERIALS

None

PROCEDURE

✓ Indicate to the group the importance of providing positive strokes to ourselves and others in order to help people feel good and increase the probability of their repetition of an appropriate behavior. Support your contention with selected quotes from Dr. Kenneth Blanchard, who suggests that we "Catch people doing something right," or Lord Chesterfield, who advised us to "Make a person like him/herself a little better and I promise s/he will like you very well indeed."

✓ Ask each person to pair up with another individual.

✓ Direct them to think of something positive that they could say to and about that person (i.e., a "one-minute praising").

✓ Then have them do it.

DISCUSSION QUESTIONS

1. How often do you deliver one-minute praisings (warm fuzzies) during the day?
2. How often do you hear others doing it?
3. How often do you *receive* one-minute praisings?
4. What do you think employee expectations are for positive feedback?
5. Why *don't* many of us give as much positive feedback as we think we should?

✓ You may wish to read one of the classically popular books dealing with the application of reinforcement principles, such as Blanchard and Johnson's *The One-Minute Manager,* or Aubray Daniel's *Bringing Out the Best in People.* The former source highlights several principles you could share with the group:

- Immediacy
- Specificity
- Solicitication of repeat behaviors
- Physical support
- Reaffirmation of overall performance

✓ By contrast, you may wish to familiarize yourself with some of the major criticisms of positive reinforcement. See, for example, Alfie Kohn's book, *Punished by Rewards.*

IF YOU HAVE MORE TIME

A few "props" can make this demonstration substantially more powerful in its impact. Simply obtain a small supply of cotton balls and one-inch squares of sandpaper. Give one of each to every member. Begin the exercise by asking them to rub some part of their body (e.g., their nose, cheek, or a knuckle) with the sandpaper and then report how it felt. Now direct them to rub a similar surface with the cotton ball and solicit their comments. Essentially, the point you are trying to make is that, inevitably, the "warm fuzzy" of the cotton ball (or praise) feels much better.

THREE TYPES OF PEOPLE

OBJECTIVE

To provide a vivid illustration of the nature of group members and their contributions to the group's overall goals

MATERIALS

Three glasses of water, 2 aspirin, 2 Bromo Seltzer tablets, and 2 Alka Seltzer tablets

PROCEDURE

✓ Explain that there are at least three types of employees in the workforce today.

- The first type usually *makes* things happen.
- The second type *watches* things as they happen.
- The third type *wonders what happened.*

Suggest that, in today's economic and competitive climate, you need more of the first type, and fewer of the others.

✓ Dramatize this key point with a simple demonstration. Pour three glasses about three-quarters full of water, and place them in view of the group. Place two aspirin in the first one and "wait" for a response. Indicate that this may represent one type of employee. Place two Bromo Seltzer in the second glass. Note that this type of employee often exhibits a great burst of initial enthusiasm, but also quickly loses it and becomes like the first. Then place two Alka Seltzer tablets in the third glass. Note that this type of employee produces a relatively strong and stable (enduring) output (and therefore is presumably the most desirable).

DISCUSSION QUESTIONS

1. Which type of employee portrayed here would you rather have on your team?
2. Is there a viable contribution that the other types can still make?
3. How can you convert one type of individual into another form?

TIPS

✓ Have a towel handy for cleaning up the results of the "fizzing."
✓ Be certain that you emphasize the potential role and value that each type of employee brings to the organization as long as they are productive. In short, one's personal style may be less important than one's accomplishments.

MAKING WORK LIKE PLAY

OBJECTIVE

To demonstrate that we sometimes take our work too seriously,
and need to explore ways to
make it "fun"

MATERIALS

None, unless you wish to use the list provided in the Comparing
Play and Work handout. Then you may wish to prepare handouts
for each participant, or have the items listed on a flip chart.

PROCEDURE

✓ Lead a brief discussion of "play" vs. "work." What are the different connotations of each? For example, what does "play
the piano" mean to a 9-year-old as compared to a concert pi-
anist? What does "playing tennis" mean to a weekend tennis
player as compared to a touring professional tennis player?

✓ Form small discussion groups of three to five persons each. Assign each group a different statement or a small number of
statements from the list on page 40.

✓ Tell them that their task is to indicate how "work" can be
made more like the elements of "play" shown there. (For example, night shift crews and day shift crews can compete for
prizes, winning performers can be named "Employee of the
Month," and so on.)

DISCUSSION QUESTIONS

1. What are the major implications of this exercise for our team?

2. What *prevents* us from making work more like play? Are these
forces real or imagined?

3. What would be the likely (positive and negative) results of
making work more like play? Could others in the organization
accept such creative behaviors and feel comfortable?

✓ To help the group focus on the issue of "play," provide a couple of examples, such as a recreational softball team.

✓ To free up their thinking, encourage them to consider the possibility of a cultural "sea change," in which all existing rules are thrown out and employees are encouraged to redesign their work systems to suit their own needs. Then be sure that you set the parameters clearly to indicate what changes you might find acceptable and which ones would not be.

IF YOU HAVE MORE TIME

Since everyone has his or her own definition of what constitutes "play," you may wish to have the group create its *own list* of the characteristics of "play" (before breaking up into discussion groups) rather than working from the list provided.

COMPARING PLAY AND WORK

Features of Play	Applications to Work
1. Alternatives are available.	**1.**
2. New games can be played on different days.	**2.**
3. Contact with equals, friends, peers.	**3.**
4. Flexibility of choosing teammates.	**4.**
5. Flexible duration of play.	**5.**
6. Flexible time of when to play.	**6.**
7. Opportunity to be/express oneself.	**7.**
8. Opportunity to use one's talents.	**8.**
9. Skillful play brings applause, praise, and recognition from spectators.	**9.**
10. Healthy competition, rivalry, and challenge exists.	**10.**
11. Opportunity for social interaction.	**11.**
12. Opportunity for ongoing teams to develop.	**12.**
13. Mechanisms for scoring one's performance are available (feedback).	**13.**
14. Rules assure basic fairness and justice.	**14.**
15. Playing involves experiences of achievement, thrill of winning, handling losing with grace, etc.	**15**

JUST A LITTLE BIT BETTER

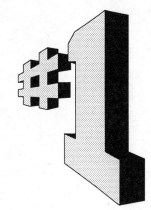

OBJECTIVE

To impress on group members that, no matter how well they are performing now, they are probably capable of doing "just a little bit better"

MATERIALS

None

PROCEDURE

✓ Ask a volunteer to step to the side of the room.

✓ Request that the person extend an arm and reach as high on the wall as possible. Be prepared to have some way to assess approximately how high the person's outstretched fingertips reached.

✓ Now ask them to extend their arm again and, by *really stretching themselves,* reach as high on the wall as they can. Note how far their fingertips extend this time (it is invariably farther).

✓ Stress a few major points from this exercise, or, preferably, ask the group to derive its own conclusions from the demonstration.

DISCUSSION QUESTIONS

1. What apprehensions do we have about doing something new or different?

2. Could *you* improve your performance in some area by 10% or more? In what areas?

3. What message might you be sending to workers when you emphasize the value of doing "just a little bit better"—such as a 10% improvement in performance at work?

4. In what ways have we "learned" to hold some portion of our energy/talent in reserve?

It can often be highly dramatic to ask the group members to note the effects of a 10% improvement in a domain highly visible to them. For example, "What might be the effects of a 10% improvement by a baseball player?" (Answer: possibly 15 more hits, 20 more total bases, several fewer errors.) In pro football, a placekicker might hit several more field goals per season, and a punter might average another four yards per kick. The impact? Substantial!

AWARENESS OF OTHERS' NEEDS

OBJECTIVE

To encourage group members to assess their sensitivity to the needs of employees

MATERIALS

One copy of the Job Factors handout for each participant, pens or pencils

PROCEDURE

✓ Distribute a copy of the Job Factors handout to each participant.

✓ Instruct them to rank-order the ten items from 1 to 10 (1 = highest, 10 = lowest) according to the degree to which workers nationwide considered that reason "very important" in deciding to take their current job. Results should be entered in column 1.

✓ Display the key on a transparency. Have participants enter the actual ranks in column 2 of their sheets, and compute the *absolute* arithmetic differences between each of their item rankings and the key (without regard to positive or negative sign) in column 3. Then ask them to add up the total.

DISCUSSION QUESTIONS

1. How accurate was each participant? (A perfect score is "0.")
2. Why might we *not* be in touch with employee needs and priorities?
3. What could each of us do to get and stay in touch?

TIPS

✓ Urge respondents to think about workers employed nationwide, not necessarily those in their own organization or unit.

✓ Invite group members to create a new set of rankings that *do* apply to your organization. Then encourage them to ask a sample of employees to complete the survey, and compare the results.

IF YOU HAVE MORE TIME

Break the participants into small groups of three to five persons and repeat the process, with the group's numbers placed in column 4. Repeat the scoring procedure, with the absolute arithmetic difference score for the group placed in column 5. Discuss:

1. Who performed better, individuals or groups?
2. What factors contribute to group success on tasks such as these?
3. How can groups be used more productively at work to capitalize on their assets?
4. What problems might groups be subject to on tasks such as these?

JOB FACTORS

Directions: Rank-order the following items from 1 to 10 (1 = highest, 10 = lowest) according to your estimate of the degree to which workers in a nationwide study reported that reason to be "very important" in deciding to take their current job.

	1	2	3	4	5
Advancement opportunity					
Control over work content					
Flexible work schedule					
Fringe benefits					
Job security					
Nature of the work					
Open communication					
Salary/wages					
Size of organization					
Stimulating work					

	Rank
Advancement opportunity	8
Control over work content	3
Flexible work schedule	7
Fringe benefits	6
Job security	4
Nature of the work	2
Open communication	1
Salary/wages	9
Size of organization	10
Stimulating work	5

Source: "Work Force Study Finds Loyalty Is Weak," *The Wall Street Journal*, September 3, 1993, p. B-1.

SUCCESS IS ...

OBJECTIVE

To demonstrate how values may change with the passage of time and acquisition of experience

MATERIALS

None

PROCEDURE

When discussing leadership, excellence, or success in any organizational setting, suggest that "success" in any venture is a highly individualistic commodity. Ask participants to think about that word "success" for a moment or two. Then follow with these questions:

✓ Think back to when you were in grade school. How did you think of success? How did you identify people you felt were successful?

✓ When you got out of school (high school or college), did these perceptions change? How?

✓ Today—right now, as we sit here—how would you identify or define success?

DISCUSSION QUESTIONS

1. How many of us as kids saw "success" primarily in the form of TV or film celebrities, or in terms of "lots of money"?

2. Did these images change much as you prepared to enter the world of work? How? Why?

3. As we finished high school or college, how many—honestly— saw success strictly as making tons of money?

4. What about now? Why do most of us perceive success in such different ways?

✓ When asking the first question (about grade school), answers typically come back as identifying celebrities, rock stars, "rich and famous" people, and the like.

✓ For the second question, expect answers in terms of monetary or material things, such as "making $___,000," "owning a BMW," and so on.

✓ For the last question, the answers will likely be more in terms of personal or professional items rather than monetary rewards.

3

Creative Problem Solving

WE'RE ALL WEALTHY!

OBJECTIVE

To provide a structured method for stimulating the generation and sharing of ideas among group members

MATERIALS

3 × 5 index cards, five for each group member

PROCEDURE

In advance of a meeting, frame a problem or issue for the group to address. Ask them to generate five of their best ideas for solving the problem and write each one on a blank card or simulated dollar bill.

Ask each participant to sign his or her name on the back of each card, to receive recognition when the ideas are shared and competitively judged. Set a deadline before the meeting for the submission of the cards.

Create a master listing of all the ideas generated, so that the group has a collective "memory" or record of the array of solutions offered.

At the beginning of the session distribute the master list. Ask each member to select the ten best ideas and mark their sheets. Take a quick count of the responses by asking for a show of hands for each item.

After you have tabulated the results, announce the best ideas, award a nominal prize, and explain how everyone is now "wealthier." They have not only stretched their minds and exercised their creative juices, but also received a large number of ideas (on the handout) that can potentially be applied to solving an organizational problem.

DISCUSSION QUESTIONS

1. What are the advantages of focusing one's mind on a problem or issue prior to the meeting?
2. How did the nature of participation in this meeting (equal generation of ideas, equal voting rights) compare with previous meetings?
3. What other problems or issues could this method be useful for?

TIPS

✓ You might try using play money instead of index cards to more clearly illustrate the "wealth" idea.
✓ If the issue addressed has broader implications, you might consider whether the results of the session (all items, or a partial list) should be communicated via a newsletter or bulletin.
✓ Be sure to give appropriate credit and recognition to *all* persons who contributed ideas.

IF YOU HAVE MORE TIME

Prior to the participants' arrival, tape all the cards to a wall (spread them out so that everyone can examine some without bumping into other observers). Ask them to examine each idea and "vote" for the ten best ideas by placing a checkmark on the bottom of the appropriate ten cards. Then collect the cards from the wall and quickly tabulate the votes to determine the highest vote-getters.

Of course, the simple generation and selection of possible solutions does not guarantee that they are well-understood or without complications. Therefore, you may wish to move the discussion further by examining the costs and benefits of the five top-rated solutions before having the group pick its overall favorite.

Another favorite approach is to list the ideas the group has generated, and give each participant an allocation of play money (e.g., 100 one dollar bills). Then ask them to allocate their money among the ideas according to how strongly they feel each proposal has merit. For example, one person might split the $100 across five equal shares, whereas another might allocate $80 to one idea and $20 to another. The idea with the greatest total "bid" is designated the "winner."

CONSULTANT FOR A MINUTE

OBJECTIVE

To brainstorm several possible solutions or suggestions for the participants' own current work challenges or problems

MATERIALS

Paper, notepads, and pencils

PROCEDURE

✓ Ask the participants to form groups of six to eight people in a circle or around tables.

✓ Each person is asked to think about a current job-related problem or concern and write it on a blank sheet of paper or on a notepad. Examples might be, "How can I get more group involvement?" or "How can I get my staff to be more punctual?"

✓ After allowing a few minutes to think about and write out their problems, ask each person to pass his/her problem to the right. That person reads the problem just received and jots down the first thought that comes to mind in addressing the problem. They are given 60 seconds to respond to the individual sheet. Monitor the time closely.

✓ Repeat this process every 60 seconds, and keep the process going until each person gets his/her own sheet back.

DISCUSSION QUESTIONS

1. Did anyone discover novel solutions that you had not previously considered?

2. Can you see any value in trying some of these suggestions?

3. Do some of these suggestions trigger other ideas or solutions for you?

4. What lesson does this teach us about reaching out to others for their assistance?

TIP

Encourage the members to select nontechnical (generic) problems that lend themselves to consultation by their colleagues.

IF YOU HAVE MORE TIME

Encourage the group to discuss some of the more practical solutions offered. What did they learn that might prove helpful to them? What alternative perspectives did they gain?

THE MIND IS A WONDERFUL THING

OBJECTIVE

To demonstrate the value of being observant about even ordinary things (like customer needs)

MATERIALS

A borrowed nondigital wrist watch

PROCEDURE

Ask someone in the group if you may borrow his or her watch for a moment. Check to be sure it is a nondigital watch, or you will need to adapt your questions.

After receiving the watch, tell that person that you would like to test his or her powers of observation, and ask the entire group to silently "play along" with the individual. Tell the loaner to assume that the watch was lost and, to reclaim it, he or she must properly identify it to the police. Then ask these sample questions, among others that might come to mind:

- What is the brand name?
- What color is the face?
- What color is the band?
- What else is printed on the face?
- Does it use roman or arabic numerals?
- Which numerals are shown?
- Does the watch have the date on it?
- Does the watch have the day on it?
- Does it have a second hand?

DISCUSSION QUESTIONS

1. How do each of you think you would have done?

2. Why aren't we more observant? (Possible answers include time pressures, lack of concern, taking things for granted, poor training, etc.)

3. Where in our organization would greater observational skills possibly pay off?

4. Have you seen incidents where people have overlooked commonplace things and problems have resulted?

5. One wag once said, "The mind is a wonderful thing. It starts working as soon as I get up in the morning, and doesn't quit until I am called upon in a group meeting." What can we do to get our minds working at the right time, when we most need them?

TIP

Remember, the point is not to embarrass the loaner of the watch. You are simply trying to make the point clear to all members: We look, but we don't always "see." We overlook a lot of rich detail, and blind ourselves to many important clues. Therefore, we need to sharpen our observational/retention skills.

IF YOU HAVE MORE TIME

If observers seem a bit smug, then give them a simple test. Ask each member to take a sheet of paper and jot the numbers 1 through 8 down the left-hand side, with space between the numbers for writing. Then ask them these eight questions:

1. What color stripe is directly under the blue field on the U.S. flag? (White)

2. If quotation marks are considered as commas, is the first pair upside down or right side up? (Upside down)

3. Is the full moon high or low in a June sky in the United States? (Low)

4. What building is shown on the five dollar U.S. bill? (Lincoln Memorial)
5. Which king on the standard playing card is shown in profile? (Diamond)
6. What is the smallest division on the standard nonmetric ruler? (1/16 inch)
7. How long is the standard cigarette? (2¾ inch)
8. Is the coin return on the right side or left side of the pay telephone? (Left)

BRAINTEASERS

OBJECTIVE

To be used as "just for fun" or when introducing the importance of creativity in TQM (total quality management) meetings

MATERIALS

Copies of the IQ Tests

PROCEDURE

✓ Hand out a copy of one of the following forms to each person.

✓ Suggest that each frame represents an adage or phrase. Their job, individually or as groups of two to three persons, is to solve the quiz.

DISCUSSION QUESTIONS

1. Did many of you find that, working as a group (i.e., a team), you arrived more easily at the answers?

2. What other ways could we use group-based creativity in our office (department, organization, etc.)?

TIPS

✓ When distributing the IQ Tests, suggest to the group that, while some of the blocks are easy to interpret, others may be more difficult. Start off by either giving the first correct answer ("hitting below the belt," for example) or by letting the group shout out the right answer.

✓ If individuals shout out an answer that is close but not exactly the "school solution," acknowledge that they're on the right track and paraphrase or give the right answer.

IQ TEST

Here are some real puzzlers for you! Decipher the hidden meaning of each set of words.

1	2	3	4
belt hitting	**EXIT** **LEG**	often not often not often	**night fly**

5	6	7	8
MIGR**A**INE	SPRIN**G** SUMME**R** AUTUM**N** WIN**T**ER	**9ALL5**	*once upon a time* N +—E S

9	10	11	12
GIVE GET GIVE GET GIVE GET GIVE GET	**breth**	ACCIDENT	**esroh riding**

13	14	15	16
EMPLOY T MEN	wire just	GRIMY SMUDGED FILTHY BESMIRCHED UNWASHED FOUL SOILED TARNISHED UNCLEAN SOOTY SULLIED DUSTY	**DO 12" OR**

ANSWERS

1. Hitting below the belt
2. Out on a limb
3. More often that not
4. Fly by night
5. A splitting headache
6. A man for all seasons
7. All in a day's work
8. Westside story
9. Forgive and forget
10. Short of breath
11. Accident prone
12. Horseback riding
13. Men out of work
14. Just under the wire
15. Dirty dozen
16. A foot in the door

IQ TEST

Here are some real puzzlers for you! Decipher the hidden meaning of each set of words.

1 C O U N T R Y C O U N T R Y	**2** 1 + T < WHOLE	**3** shrif	**4** GRATIS ALL ALL ALL ALL
5 THE SAND	**6** COLLAR 102°	**7** to ngue ngue	**8** COLT Jr.
9 NOW IN HERE	**10** hoRN	**11** [income]	**12** D DUMP D U goose U M feathers M P DUMP P
13 ME ——— IT IT IT IT IT IT IT IT IT IT IT	**14** ACUM	**15** GAG U	**16** L✗EAST

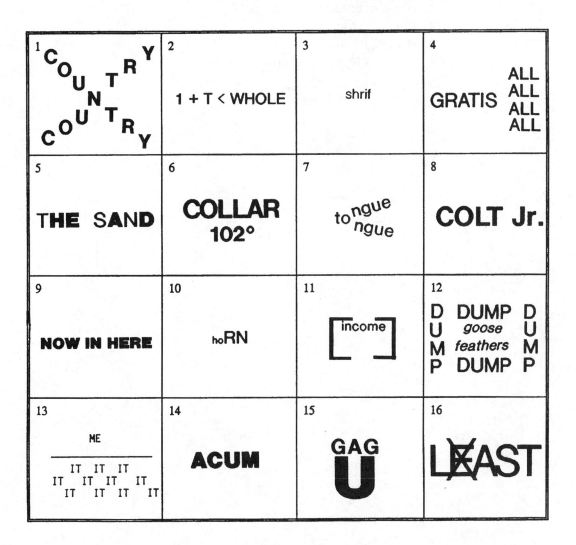

61

ANSWERS

1. Cross country
2. The whole is greater than the sum of its parts
3. Short shrift
4. Free for all
5. Head in the sand
6. Hot under the collar
7. Forked tongue or tongue twister
8. Son of a gun
9. Nowhere in sight
10. Little Big Horn
11. High income brackets
12. Down in the dumps
13. It's below me.
14. See you in the morning.
15. The gag's on you.
16. Last but not least

IQ TEST

Here are some real puzzlers for you! Decipher the hidden meaning of each set of words.

1 L^{E}S$_O$D^{U}B **TENNIS**	**2** timing tim ing	**3** **JJJ BBB**	**4** 1/4 1/4 1/4 1/4 1/4
5 hand hand hand deck	**6** e e q u a l s m c	**7** *goodbye*	**8** **DR. DR.**
9 dipping	**10** **fighting**	**11** S O E S H W R	**12** **GGES EGSG** **GEGS SEGG**
13 HEAD SHOULDERS ARMS BODY LEGS ANKLES FEET TOES	**14** **K A N E L**	**15** a chance n	**16** THE END ↑

ANSWERS

1. Mixed doubles tennis
2. Split second timing
3. The birds and the bees
4. Close quarters
5. All hands on deck.
6. $E = MC^2$
7. Waving goodbye
8. A paradox
9. Skinny dipping
10. Two black eyes
11. Scattered showers
12. Scrambled eggs
13. Head and shoulders above the rest
14. Twisted ankle
15. An outside chance
16. Beginning of the end

IQ TEST

Here are some real puzzlers for you! Decipher the hidden meaning of each set of words.

1 PERSON PERSONS PERSONS PERSONS	**2** Insult + injury	**3** EVARELTO	**4** (S T E A K)^3
5 NO WAYS IT WAYS	**6** ALL world	**7** $\underline{1\ 3\ 5\ 7\ 9}$ WHELMING	**8** **CCCCCCC**
9 **gettingitall**	**10** **alai**	**11** **CUS TOM**	**12** **MAUD**
13 $\dfrac{\text{T} \atop \text{T} \atop +\text{T}}{\text{3T}}$	**14** **RASINGINGIN**	**15** FAIRY WOLF DUCKLING	**16** **24 Hours**

ANSWERS

1. First person singular
2. Add insult to injury.
3. Elevator out of order
4. Cubed steak
5. No two ways about it
6. It's a small world after all.
7. The odds are overwhelming.
8. High seas
9. Getting it all together
10. Jai (high) alai
11. A break in custom
12. Mad about you
13. Teetotaler
14. Singing in the rain
15. The good, the bad, the ugly
16. Call it a day.

IQ TEST

Here are some real puzzlers for you! Decipher the hidden meaning of each set of words.

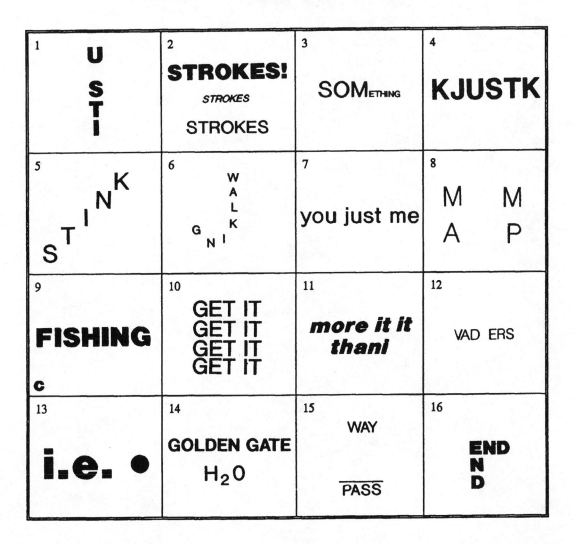

1 U S T I T	**2** **STROKES!** *STROKES* STROKES	**3** SOM_{ETHING}	**4** **KJUSTK**
5 S T I N K S	**6** W A L K G N I	**7** you just me	**8** M M A P
9 **FISHING** c	**10** GET IT GET IT GET IT GET IT	**11** *more it it thani*	**12** VAD ERS
13 **i.e.** ●	**14** **GOLDEN GATE** H_2O	**15** WAY ――― PASS	**16** **END** **N** **D**

ANSWERS

1. It's up to you.
2. Different strokes
3. The start of something big
4. Just in case
5. Fouled up
6. Jay walking
7. Just between you and me
8. Time's up.
9. Deep sea fishing
10. Forget it.
11. More to it than meets the eye
12. Space invaders
13. That is beside the point.
14. Water under the bridge
15. Highway overpass
16. Making ends meet

OUTSIDE THE BOX

OBJECTIVE

To illustrate the importance of going "outside the box" and continually looking for creative ways to solve problems

MATERIALS

Paper, pens or pencils, flip chart, transparency, overhead projector or handout of the Nine Dots Puzzle

PROCEDURE

✓ Show (or draw) the nine dots puzzle and ask the group to draw a similar illustration on paper.

✓ Then give these instructions: "Without taking pen or pencil off your paper, please connect all nine dots with four continuous straight lines."

✓ Because this exercise has been in use for some time, pause for a moment after you give the instructions, and ask, "How many of you have seen this before and can do it with four straight lines?" As they raise their hands, tell them, "Great! Then you do it with three straight lines." If you still see some "knowing" faces, say, "If you can do it with three, then do it with one straight line."

DISCUSSION QUESTIONS

1. If you had difficulty solving the puzzle, what were some of the constraints?

2. Don't we often find ourselves "boxed in" on certain projects? How can we get "outside" the box?

3. What are some other ways to connect all nine dots with just one line? (Use a wide brush; fold the paper so that all nine dots are partially superimposed; go over and around the paper, etc.)

✓ As indicated, some people may give you a quick nonverbal response of already knowing the answer. Then with a smile, ask them to do it with *three* lines. This usually gets their attention back.

✓ After the exercise, ask someone to show the group how they got the four lines, then the three lines, and finally *one* line.

NINE DOTS PUZZLE

Directions: With four straight lines and without taking pen or pencil off the paper, connect all nine dots.

NINE DOTS PUZZLE

Solution: (1) Start at the far left corner of the top row, and continue straight to the right side (outside the box!). (2) Draw diagonally to the lower left side. (3) Then draw straight up to the top left corner. (4) Draw diagonally to connect all nine dots.

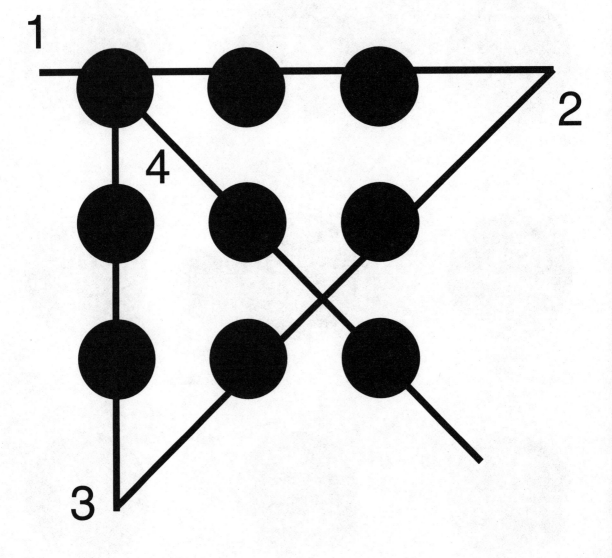

NINE DOTS PUZZLE

Alternate Solution: Using three straight lines: (1) Start at the upper edge of the left circle in the top row, and draw diagonally (outside the box!). (2) Then go back to the left. (3) Finally go to the right.

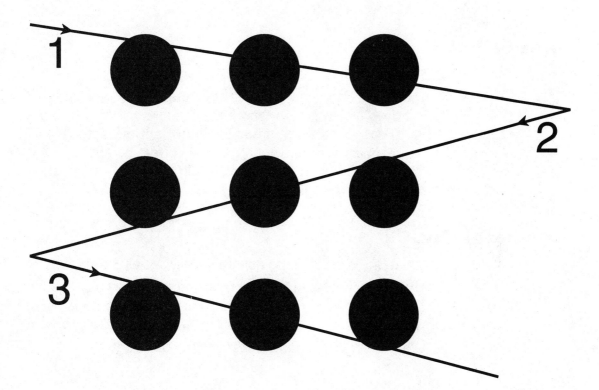

COUNT THE SQUARES

OBJECTIVE

To encourage people to "see" different parts of a problem and to look at things from different perspectives

MATERIALS

Flip chart, transparency, overhead projector or handout of Hidden Squares

PROCEDURE

✓ Show the group the picture of the large square.

✓ Then ask, "How many squares are there?" As people begin to call out "16," ask, "Any more?" Someone will quickly shout "17." "Any more?" The group begins to "get the picture," and the numbers keep growing until the correct number of 32 is reached (16 individual squares, 1 big square, 11 squares of four each and 4 squares of 9 each).

DISCUSSION QUESTIONS

1. What blocked our being able to initially see all 32 squares?
2. Have you ever faced a problem that seemed too big (i.e., big square), but as you solved or took parts (individual squares) of the big problem away, the problem seemed easy to solve?
3. What other things can we learn from this example?

TIPS

✓ Use a transparency or figure large enough to be easily seen by the group.

✓ After the first few responses of "16" are given, keep asking for more. Some people will need help in being able to dissect the square to be able to see all 32 squares.

✓ If someone challenges that there are actually more than 32, compliment them and agree that there are, indeed, more than 32. For example, the 25 points of intersection joining each square is also a square, etc.

WHAT IF?

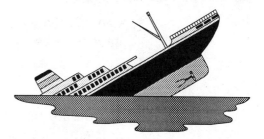

OBJECTIVE

To allow people to pre-
pare contingency plans
for emergency or poten-
tially serious situations

MATERIALS

Nerf ball

PROCEDURE

✓ After a brief review of the rules for brainstorming (i.e., no
criticism, quantity not quality, wild ideas are OK, and
hitchhiking), tell the group they will now have a chance to
do some advance thinking on handling potential future
problems.

✓ Break the larger group into subgroups of three or four
people.

✓ Ask them to think of a recent experience in which Murphy's
law was a player. This could be a situation that they personally experienced or that they may have heard about from a co-
worker. Have each group agree on one problem, such as "Half
of my people called in sick on the same day," or "I couldn't
find my notes as I was about to give a talk."

✓ Call on one group to identify their problem situation. They do
so by saying, "What if … [half of my people called in sick on
the same day]?" Give them the Nerf ball as they state their
problem. They then throw the Nerf ball to another group.
Whoever catches the ball must offer several quick solutions to
the question posed. After the responding group runs out of
answers, let others also make suggestions.

✓ After a few minutes of possible answers are provided, the Nerf
ball is then tossed to another group and the process is repeat-
ed. Continue as time allows.

DISCUSSION QUESTION

1. Can you see the importance of this Monday morning quarter-backing? Have some of you experienced similar situations?

TIPS

✓ The group may need initial prodding in thinking up recent problems. Have two or three examples to spur their thinking.

✓ After some responses are given, ask the person who had the original problem how he or she actually handled the situation.

BRAINSTORMING REVISITED

OBJECTIVE

To show the relevance of a time-tested creative exercise in its application for TQM or any other problem-solving activity

MATERIALS

Paper, pens or pencils

PROCEDURE

Although the brainstorming process has been around for a number of years, it is regaining its popularity in problem-solving meetings. Because many people have never been exposed to this novel approach, review and describe the four basic rules of this system:

1. No critical judgment is allowed.

2. Quantity, not quality, is desired.

3. "Free-wheeling" is welcomed—the wider, the better!

4. Combination and improvement are sought.

✓ To get participants in a creative mode, use some type of warm-up activity before delving into the real-world problem to be discussed.

✓ This could take the form of asking each group to come up with as many ideas as they can for using a paper clip. Allow the group only 60 seconds for this, and ask one person in each group to simply jot down the number of ideas (not writing down the actual ideas).

✓ Following this fun activity, move into the problem at hand.

✓ Form groups of five to seven people for each brainstorm session.

PACK UP YOUR TROUBLES ...

OBJECTIVE

To allow people to "let go" of continuing distracting concerns or problems, at the same time providing a vehicle to enable other team members or colleagues to suggest solutions to those issues

MATERIALS

Paper and pencils, empty receptacles or wastebaskets

PROCEDURE

This activity can be used at any time during a regular staff or departmental meeting, team meeting, or any other type of meeting.

✓ Introduce the exercise by acknowledging that most of us tend to have "nagging" problems or concerns, or other distractions that just won't go away. Tell your group that this is the time to "pack up" those problems and "toss" them away for a while.

✓ Ask each person to think of such a problem or concern—either on the topic or subject being discussed or on any other general issue that is bothering them. Caution against items of a personal nature, e.g., "too much month left at the end of the money," disagreements with spouses or partners, etc.

✓ Each person then writes his/her problem on a notepad or sheet of paper. They then "pack up" their troubles, i.e., crumple up the papers, and toss them into the wastebasket.

✓ After all the papers are in receptacles, form groups of three, and have one person from each group pick out a crumpled sheet from the basket.

✓ The trio now "owns" that problem and is given three minutes to write down and discuss as many possible solutions as they can in that time frame.

✓ Each group then reads their problem to the group and reports their solutions. Solicit additional suggestions from others in attendance.

✓ Repeat this process as time allows or until all problems are addressed.

NO TIME TO WASTE

OBJECTIVE

To give people a chance to think about the many and varied time wasters in today's office, and how they might be lessened

MATERIALS

Transparency, overhead, copies of the Time Wasters handout paper, and pens or pencils

PROCEDURE

✓ Ask the group to think about "time" and how some days seem to fly by and little gets done. Certainly, none of us are immune to people, places, or things that just seem to get in the way of our work.

✓ With this in mind, have individuals write down their "Top Ten" list of typical time wasters.

✓ After a few minutes, form groups of three and synthesize lists to see which ones are common to many of us.

✓ Then show the overhead transparency and elicit discussion as to how these (as well as their own listing) might be overcome.

DISCUSSION QUESTIONS

1. How did your group's answers compare to the list shown?

2. What are the three biggest time wasters in your area?

3. What are some creative ways we can overcome them?

TIPS

✓ Depending on the organization, the "top ten" Time Wasters handout may not at all resemble the group's answers. Acknowledge that and spend more time on the group's list.

✓ Solicit some concrete suggestions on overcoming the major issues.

1. Crises

2. Telephone calls

3. Poor planning

4. Attempting to do too much

5. Drop-in visitors

6. Poor delegation

7. Personal disorganization

8. Lack of self-discipline

9. Inability to say "no"

10. Procrastination

4

Managing Change: Dealing with Resistance and Getting Buy-in

PERCEPTUAL BARRIERS TO CHANGE

OBJECTIVE

To demonstrate that it is important to identify and realistically assess the factors limiting our success

MATERIALS

None, other than the Nature of Constraints handout

PROCEDURE

✓ Relate the story of the northern pike that was placed in one-half of a large table-aquarium, with numerous minnows swimming freely (and visibly) in the other half of the glass-divided tank. As the pike became hungrier, it made numerous unsuccessful efforts to obtain the minnows, but only succeeded in battering its snout against the glass divider. Slowly the pike "learns" that reaching the minnows is an impossible task, and seemingly resigns itself to its fate. When the glass partition is carefully removed, the pike (surprisingly?) does not attack the minnows, even though they swim bravely around it. This illustrates the *pike syndrome,* which is characterized by:

- Ignoring differences in situations
- Assuming complete knowledge
- Overgeneralizing reactions
- Rigid commitment to the past
- Refusal to consider alternatives
- Inability to function under stress
- Feeling victimized by one's environment
- Failing to test one's perceived constraints

✓ Then engage the group in a discussion of the following questions and issues.

DISCUSSION QUESTIONS

1. What are some examples of people who have exhibited the *pike syndrome*?

2. How can we help others (or ourselves) break out of these mental traps?

3. What kinds of behaviors would you like to start or stop doing?

4. What are some of the perceptual constraints that operate in our workplace?

5. How can we learn to more realistically assess the nature of our constraints?

TIPS

✓ Have an example from your life available to demonstrate the classification of constraints to the group so as to stimulate their thinking.

✓ You might also invite the group to generate a list of skills and behaviors that would be useful to develop as either preventatives or antidotes to the *pike syndrome.*

IF YOU HAVE MORE TIME

✓ Explain that the constraints that seemingly box us in may sometimes be created by our own perceptions of the limitations in our environment. Demonstrate this by asking each person to think of one thing that they would like to start or stop doing. Tell them to list all the things that now prevent them from accomplishing their objective. Then show them the figure provided, and ask them to categorize their own list of constraints according to whether they are basically real or illusionary, and whether they are rigid or flexible. Both the illusionary and the flexible types can at least be explored, if not changed; only the Type B constraints (real and rigid) represent unyielding obstacles.

✓ When they are done, point out that one organization (General Electric) discovered that over 95% of the constraints identified by its first-line supervisors were classified as either flexible or illusionary. In short, it would be useful for everyone to test their limits, be willing to experiment, take some risks, and make sure that they have accurately assessed their own environment.

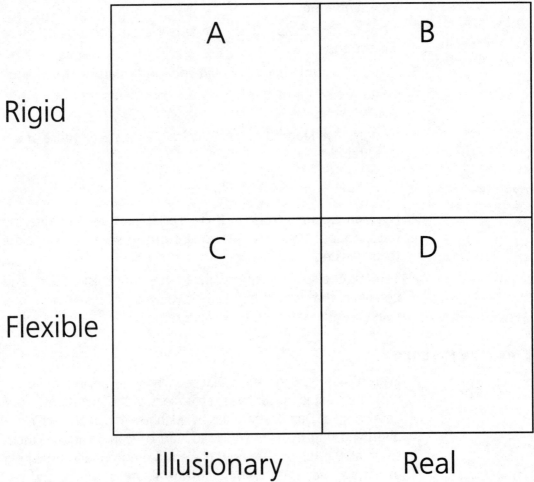

Rigid

Flexible

Illusionary   Real

ACTION PLANNING FOR CHANGES

OBJECTIVE

To introduce group members to an approach to change called the force-field technique

MATERIALS

Copies of the Action Plan handout, pens or pencils

PROCEDURE

✓ Distribute copies of the Action Plan to each participant.

✓ Explain that this tool is called force-field analysis.

✓ Talk them through the form so that they can use it later independently.

- *Goal:* Specify what they want to change or accomplish. For example, "Reduce unexcused absenteeism by 10% in the next ten weeks."

- *Driving forces:* List the items that are "pushing" the change or action, e.g., "The boss says so."

- *Restraining forces:* Write out the factors that tend to hold back or block the change from taking place, e.g., "Not enough resources."

DISCUSSION QUESTIONS

1. In what ways can this tool be useful to you?
2. What are its shortcomings?
3. What suggestions can you make for revising or adapting it?

TIPS

Don't let the group stop with their *analysis* of the driving and restraining forces. Suggest to the group that for change to be successfully made, one or more restraining forces must be removed or lessened. Have the group suggest ways of doing so for the items listed. Then encourage them to *use* the force-field analysis method in the near future.

IF YOU HAVE MORE TIME

If you can afford more discussion time, have them address these issues:

✓ *Timetable:* Actually write out some interim dates and commit to the actions being done.
✓ *Commitment:* State exactly what priority these changes or actions have and how committed you are to seeing them through to their completion.

ACTION PLAN

1. GOAL (What do you want to do/accomplish?):

_____

_____

_____

2. DRIVING FORCES:

A. _____

B. _____

C. _____

3. RESTRAINING FORCES:

A. _____

B. _____

C. _____

4. ACTION PLAN:

A. _____

B. _____

C. _____

CONFRONTING MYTHS

It'll only take a minute to fix this.

OBJECTIVE

To show that it is easy to hold mistaken perceptions about a topic

MATERIALS

None, unless you want to display the Myth List visually or distribute it as a printed handout

PROCEDURE

✓ Define "myth" for the group: a fiction or half-truth that appeals to the consciousness of people while expressing some of their deep, commonly felt emotions.

✓ Progressively disclose to them some common myths in our society today, such as:

- One size fits all.
- You're only as old as you feel.
- The check is in the mail.
- I'll still respect you in the morning.
- I'm from the government, and I'm here to help you.
- It'll only take a minute to fix this.
- There's nothing *really* wrong with you.
- There is no discrimination in this organization.
- Everybody is doing it this way.

✓ Then add one or more myths pertinent to the topic of the current meeting, such as:

- Once a customer sees our new product, it will sell itself.
- Our new procedure for doing this is much easier (or simpler, faster, cheaper) than before.

✓ Then proceed to focus on that myth by asking the following questions.

DISCUSSION QUESTIONS

1. Where might this myth have come from?
2. What factors contribute to its perpetuation?
3. What can we do to dispel this myth?
4. Is it indeed a myth, or is there a large measure of truth to it?

TIPS

✓ You may wish to relate a corporate story to the group, detailing how the existence of a myth led to an earlier failure.

✓ Obtain and show a video of Joel Barker, who vividly demonstrates how clinging to outmoded paradigms (which are essentially myths) led some companies into tailspins.

✓ Where appropriate, bring in "props" to demonstrate that the myth is indeed false. For example, comparing your product to a competitor's product might powerfully prove the falsehood of a myth.

IF YOU HAVE MORE TIME

✓ Disclose only one or two of the myths listed in Procedures, and instead invite the group to generate their own list. This is a useful technique to stimulate their creative juices, and provides an opportunity to introduce a bit of humor into the team's discussion.

✓ You may wish to make this a regular (periodic) topic to revisit by letting the group generate (and subsequently add to) a longer list of organizational myths that need to be addressed.

One size fits all.

You're only as old as you feel.

The check is in the mail.

I'll still respect you in the morning.

I'm from the government, and I'm here to help you.

It'll only take a minute to fix this.

There's nothing *really* wrong with you.

There is no discrimination in this organization.

Everybody is doing it this way.

MANAGING CHANGE

OBJECTIVE

To provide the group with an opportunity to study the process of change and show how resistance might be lessened in the future

MATERIALS

Flip chart, paper, pens or pencils

PROCEDURE

✓ Divide the group into subsets of four to five people, preferably from different departments or offices.

✓ Then ask the groups to discuss these questions with their team members.

- Think of a recent situation in which some kind of change was brought forth in your office (department, firm, etc.). Discuss.
- Was that change resisted?
- Why (or why not)?
- Looking back, what might have made that change easier to buy into (or to sell)?

✓ Allow sufficient time for discussion. Then solicit random reports.

DISCUSSION QUESTIONS

1. Did you find similarity in any of your changes?
2. How many of you found no resistance to the change? Tell us about it.
3. Why is change so often resisted?
4. What are some of the things that might make your next change easier to sell (or buy into)?

✓ If group members are from different areas of the organization, the activity will produce better results. If group members are all from the same office, it may be an exercise where finger pointing and other counterproductive behaviors reveal themselves.

✓ Have each group agree on only one change to discuss. However, if time allows, secure additional comments.

CHANGE IS THE NAME OF THIS GAME

OBJECTIVE

To allow group to experience—first hand—the effects of change

MATERIALS

None

PROCEDURE

✓ After a brief discussion on the continual changes we all see in everyday situations, suggest that the best way to really understand change is to actually experience it.

✓ Ask the group to stand and have everyone find a partner forming groups of two. After everyone is paired up, tell the group to take just a moment and simply observe the partner, i.e., what he/she is wearing, jewelry, color of shoes, etc.

✓ Call time after just one minute and ask each person to turn and face away from the partner. As each person is facing the other way, ask them to change four or five things about their appearance, i.e., take off their glasses, move their watch to the other arm, loosen a tie, etc.

✓ After a minute or so, tell them to turn and once again face their partners and see if they can identify the changes that were made. After so doing, ask them to take their seats.

DISCUSSION QUESTIONS

1. How many of you felt a bit uncomfortable when staring at the other person? How did you feel being so closely observed yourself?

2. How many have a difficult time changing even four or five things about your appearance?

3. How many—right now—have gone back to the exact way you were before the change? Discuss.

This activity is best used when introducing an internal change in the organization or when discussing the topic of change in a staff or team meeting.

SEARCHING FOR QUALITY

OBJECTIVE

To stimulate thinking about quality, and the impact of mindsets like "That's good enough for me," or "The customer doesn't expect any more than that"

MATERIALS

Handout or overhead transparency of If 99.9% Is Good Enough, Then …

PROCEDURE

✓ Ask participants what quality level, expressed as a percentage of total items produced, they would accept if they were placed in charge of a product line or service. On a flip chart or whiteboard, write the following table:

Level	Number of Responses
95%?	
96%?	
97%?	
98%?	
99%?	

✓ Poll them, by a show of hands, as to the level acceptable to them.

✓ Then indicate that some contemporary firms have sought to hold their reject rates down to just 1/10th of 1 percent (99.9% quality)! Ask them if they think 99.9% quality is adequate.

✓ Finally, illustrate some of the effects of even a 99.9% quality level by progressively revealing the startling statistics on the handout.

DISCUSSION QUESTIONS

1. Would *you* still be satisfied with 99.9% quality in those areas?

2. Should our *customers* be satisfied at that level?

3. What are the major *impediments* to higher quality in our area?

4. What can we do to increase the quality of *our* product or service?

TIP

Inform them of Motorola's commitment to achieve Six Sigma quality levels—fewer than 3 rejects per million items produced!

IF YOU HAVE MORE TIME

✓ Ask the group what "tools" are available to them for aiding in the improvement of quality. Have these tools been shared across all members?

✓ Form small discussion groups to brainstorm ways to obtain improvements in quality levels.

12 newborns will be given to the wrong parents daily.

114,500 mismatched pairs of shoes will be shipped/year.

18,322 pieces of mail will be mishandled/hour.

2,000,000 documents will be lost by the IRS this year.

2.5 million books will be shipped with the wrong covers.

Two planes landed at Chicago's O'Hare airport will be unsafe every day.

315 entries in *Webster's Dictionary* will be misspelled.

20,000 incorrect drug prescriptions will be written this year.

880,000 credit cards in circulation will turn out to have incorrect cardholder information on their magnetic strips.

103,260 income tax returns will be processed incorrectly during the year.

5.5 million cases of soft drinks produced will be flat.

291 pacemaker operations will be performed incorrectly.

3056 copies of tomorrow's *Wall Street Journal* will be missing one of the three sections.

5

Surfacing Hidden
On-the-Job Problems

I WISH, I WISH

OBJECTIVE

To determine potential problem areas in an organization

MATERIALS

None

PROCEDURE

✓ When doing personal interviews, either formal or informal, with co-workers or colleagues, ask: "If you had a 'wish list' and could change anything about your job, what would it be?"

✓ Make notes during the discussion, and continue as necessary to uncover—or discover—areas that may be in need of attention.

DISCUSSION QUESTIONS

1. What do you like best about your job?
2. If you were "king/queen" for the day, what would you change in the company (your job, your office, the entire organization)?
3. What should we be doing to make your job easier? More productive?
4. What would your boss make as his/her wish?
5. What new equipment or materials do you wish you had?

TIPS

✓ This exercise must be done in an atmosphere of trust and openness.

✓ Ensure that the individual understands this is not a "witch-hunt," but a sincere way to learn how areas might be improved.

TEN SIMPLE QUESTIONS?

OBJECTIVES

To encourage group members to be alert to tiny details, dangerous assumptions, and the importance of careful reading that hold the key to success

MATERIALS

Transparency or handout of Ten Simple Questions, paper, pens or pencils

PROCEDURE

✓ Present the Ten Simple Questions quiz, allowing a very tight time limit (e.g., 3 minutes).

✓ Before you give them the correct answers, ask them how many had the (most likely) *incorrect* answer for each one (e.g., 13 hours and 45 minutes for question 1; 4 [September, April, June, and November] for question 2; 11 for question 3).

✓ Then present the answers to them, and lead a discussion.

Key:

1. 1 hour, 45 minutes
2. 11 months (all but February)
3. 7 pigs lived
4. 157 (3 × 50, + 7)
5. 10 (9 fielders + 1 batter); 13 (9 + 1 batter + 3 baserunners). Add 1 if you count the on-deck batter.
6. "In God We Trust" or "United States of America"
7. Two hours (now, + 4 half-hours)
8. The match
9. They aren't playing each other.
10. "Mispelled" is misspelled.

DISCUSSION QUESTIONS

1. What factors caused you to err?
2. How might those factors affect your work performance?
3. What can you do to control (minimize or eliminate) such factors?

TIPS

This type of game can be deflating to some individuals who have strong self-images, and they may become defensive. Therefore, you must carefully decide whether to ask for individual reports of success on the exercise (e.g., number incorrect or correct). The purpose is not to make participants look or feel badly, but to alert them to the necessity of reading carefully, noting small but important factors, and not making improper assumptions.

IF YOU HAVE MORE TIME

After the individual members have had a chance to answer the questions (but before providing the answer key), you may wish to break the total group into small groups to collaborate on their responses.

TEN SIMPLE QUESTIONS

1. Being very tired, a child went to bed at 7:00 o'clock at night. The child had a morning piano lesson, and therefore set the alarm clock to ring at 8:45. How many hours and minutes of sleep could the child get? _____

2. Some months (like October) have 31 days. Only February has precisely 28 (except in a leap year). How many months have 30 days? _____

3. A farmer had 18 pigs, and all but 7 died. How many were left? _____

4. Divide 50 by 1/3, and add 7. What is the answer? _____

5. What is the minimum number of active baseball players on the playing field during any part of an inning? _____ Maximum? _____

6. What four words appear on every denomination of U.S. currency? _____ _____ _____ _____

7. If a physician gave you five pills and told you to take one every half-hour, how long would your supply last? _____

8. If you had only one match and entered a cold, dimly lit room where there was a kerosene lamp, an oil heater, and a wood-burning stove, which would you light first?

_____

9. Two women play checkers. They play five games without a draw game, and each woman wins the same number of games. How can this be? _____

10. What word is mispelled in this test? _____

PORTRAIT OF MY JOB

OBJECTIVE

To get a perception (individually or collectively) of how people may see their respective jobs

MATERIALS

Paper, pens or pencils, flip charts, and markers

PROCEDURE

✓ Break into groups of three or four people and ask each person to individually sketch out a picture of how they "see" their jobs. Ask them to be novel in their approach. They can use metaphors, analogies, TV shows, movies, sports, etc. that describe the job.

✓ Groups then draw each illustration on flip charts.

DISCUSSION QUESTIONS

1. How do you really "see" your job?
2. How does your job fit in with the big picture?
3. Has your perception changed recently? How? Why?
4. How would your customers (or colleagues) see your organization?

TIPS

✓ Because individuals may need some help initially, provide them with sample illustrations. For example, "I see my job as a three-ring circus …," or a picture is drawn of a desk with an in-basket ten feet high, and so on.

✓ Tell the group that no extra credit is given for artistic ability. We're interested in their perceptions.

OUR CUSTOMER IS WEALTHY

OBJECTIVES

To accent the "wealth" that exists in customers if group members will just look for it

MATERIALS

Transparency made from the master word list on page 111 that shows some (but not all) of the possibilities for the word "customer," paper, and pens or pencils

PROCEDURE

✓ Indicate to members that their task, working alone, is to identify as many legitimate words as they can from the letters available to them in the word "customer," using each only once. Ask them to make two predictions first—the number of words they will *individually* identify, and the word score of the *highest producer.*

✓ Then give them a tight time limit (e.g., 5 minutes) and set them loose on the task.

DISCUSSION QUESTIONS

1. How many words did you predict you'd find? How does your own performance expectation compare with the expectations others held for themselves?

2. Did you exceed your own expectations or fall short? Why?

3. How many words did you predict could be found? How does this compare to the actual total?

4. How do you explain the actual results?

5. What does this exercise illustrate to you? ("Customers" are a rich source of information.)

6. In what ways are we mining (or could we mine) our customers for greater wealth?

TIPS

The example used here to illustrate the exercise is "customer." However, you could use *any* key word that is relevant to your current agenda.

IF YOU HAVE MORE TIME

Instead of an individual approach (or following it), form teams and structure a game in which they must find either words of 3, 4, 5, 6, or 7 letters only or words beginning only with a certain letter, such as t, o, c, u, r, or m.

Us	Ore	Or
Ort	Use	User
Rest	Rut	Rot
Rote	Rose	Cot
Cost	Cote	Come
Comer	Comes	Course
Cut	Cur	Core
Corset	Court	Sum
Some	Sore	Sot
Sour	Set	To
Tome	Tore	Tomes
To	Me	More
Mouse	Met	Must
Most	Toes	Tour
Custom	Costume	Costumer
Emu		

6

Team-Building Exercises

THE JIGSAW PUZZLE

OBJECTIVE

To teach team members a new metaphor for teamwork: the jigsaw puzzle!

MATERIALS

✓ Transparency or handout of jigsaw pieces or, as a richer alternative, pieces of an actual puzzle to look at and work with

✓ Flip chart and markers

PROCEDURE

✓ Show, or distribute a handout of, the pieces of a jigsaw puzzle to the group.

✓ Ask them to list all the ways in which the jigsaw is *similar* to the composition and operation of a highly effective work group or team. (*Hint:* It may be useful for you to provide them with a simple example, to start their thought processes going. An illustration you might share with them is "Role clarity: Each piece plays a specific role in the eventual solution.")

✓ Record their responses on a flip chart for all to see. Some of the many possibilities include:

- There are *boundaries* (the straight-edged pieces).
- When completed, there are *no gaps* in the product.
- Pieces are highly *interconnected.*
- Each piece is *unique* in its nature (similar to the individual differences among people).
- The solution is a *fragile* one (easily broken).
- The whole is *more than* (different from) *the sum* of its parts.
- Some pieces are *central,* some peripheral.
- There are *"natural"* groupings (e.g., by color).

- Pieces need someone to *move* them (e.g., motivate, or make job assignments).
- A rapid solution is aided by someone with an *overall vision* of the product.

DISCUSSION QUESTIONS

1. Are you surprised by the number of similarities?
2. What are the ways in which we can use this metaphor within our group or team?
3. What action guidelines does this point toward?
4. What can each of us do to make progress toward our becoming a highly effective team?

TIPS

✓ An alternative is to create two subgroups and ask each of them to work on either the similarity or the difference questions (see below) so that both sets of answers get generated at the same time.

✓ After creation of the list of similarities, ask the group to assess itself against that list of characteristics, and then create an action plan for improvement.

✓ Refer frequently to the Jigsaw Puzzle in future meetings to remind them of the critical characteristics of high-performing teams, perhaps focusing on a single characteristic for a week (or month) at a time. This serves to reinforce the discussion.

IF YOU HAVE MORE TIME

Ask them to describe the ways in which the jigsaw puzzle is *different* from a highly effective team. List these on a separate sheet of flip chart paper. Some of the many possibilities include:

- Pieces are *not interchangeable.*
- Pieces are fixed in size, shape, and color, and therefore *cannot bend and adapt.*
- Total product (puzzle) is *limited* in what it can be by the nature of the present pieces.

IS IT A "GO" OR "NO GO"?

OBJECTIVE

To help a group leader discover whether there is truly "consensus" among the participants

MATERIALS

An adequate supply of "signal cards"

PROCEDURE

This procedure helps to combat one of the greatest dangers in group decision making—the false assumption that a consensus has been reached because "no one spoke up." You *need* to know whether the group supports ("go") or does not ("no go") support a proposal before proceeding with it.

✓ Before the session, create "signal cards" that can be used to send nonverbal messages from members to you. One option is to obtain poster boards that are, say, red on one side and green on the other. Cut them up into 3-inch squares.

✓ At the beginning of the session, distribute one square of each color to each participant.

✓ Ask them to display a colored card—either continuously or periodically in response to direct questions. The green cards should be displayed when they agree with an emerging conclusion (or pace of discussion). The red cards should be shown when they are opposed to a proposed action or are dissatisfied with the pace or direction of discussion. You may want to provide additional cards for other signals—such as white for neutrality or yellow for uncertainty.

DISCUSSION QUESTIONS

1. What is the meaning of "consensus"?

2. How important is it to discover what others are thinking and feeling?

3. What responsibility do we have for soliciting this information? For acting on it?

TIPS

✓ It will likely take a few reminders for the group to become familiar with, and willing to use, this procedure. However, they will soon remember to display the proper card if you call on someone to explain their concerns and they discover that they have mistakenly left their "red card" on display.

✓ The key is to use the procedure regularly, and not just on rare occasions. It can be a highly effective way for the group leader to obtain either subtle or not-so-subtle cues from the group about their reactions to a topic or progress on it.

✓ Think carefully about the form of questions you plan to ask. The "cleanest" ones have a yes/no or true/false or agree/disagree response pattern to them.

✓ Remind the group that the signal cards are not just for your benefit. They, too, can look around the room to find out what others are thinking.

IF YOU HAVE MORE TIME

You might also consider creating sets of Olympic-style judging cards (e.g., 10, 9, 8, ...) for each member. Then, in response to a question that probes for the degree of agreement or support, you can obtain a quick assessment of the *potency* of their feelings.

WHAT'S IN (ON) A PENNY?

OBJECTIVES

✓ To highlight the value of group (team) efforts
✓ To demonstrate the importance of details

MATERIALS

Front View, Back View, and Features of a Penny handouts, paper, and pens or pencils

PROCEDURE

✓ Ask group members, working individually, to list all the distinguishable characteristics of a common penny.
✓ Have them compare their individual and group lists with the master list (and/or the visual sketch) provided.
  - Record, through a show of hands, how many individuals scored each item correctly.
  - Compute the average individual score, and prepare a visual tally of the range of results. Award a token "prize" to the person with the most items listed.

DISCUSSION QUESTIONS

1. How can individuals see something as common as a penny almost daily, yet not "see" its characteristics?
2. How can we *increase* our individual (and daily) attention to important details?
3. To what degree is it true in your jobs that "It's the little things [like forgotten characteristics of a penny] that will get you"? How might this be true in supplier or customer relationships?

✓ Place a tight time limit on the brainstorming/listing period.

✓ Stress that it is the *principle* to be gained (and later applied) from the exercise that is important, not the (penny) task itself.

✓ You may wish to try a more visual approach (especially if you are dealing with, or wish to stimulate the reactions of, left-brained people). If so, provide them with large cutouts of a blank penny on which they can write or draw the major characteristics of a penny.

IF YOU HAVE MORE TIME

After they have generated their individual lists, divide the members into groups. Have them share their lists, compare them to each other's, and, by brainstorming, develop a new master list of characteristics. Then record, through a show of hands from a spokesperson for each group, how many groups scored each item correctly. Then ask, "What does this tell you about the value of team (or at least pooled individual) efforts?"

LIBERTY

IN GOD WE TRUST

1979

FEATURES OF A PENNY

<u>FRONT SIDE</u>:
1. "In God We Trust"
2. "Liberty"
3. Date
4. Mint mark (under date, sometimes)
5. President Lincoln's portrait facing to his left

<u>BACK SIDE</u>:
6. "United States of America"
7. "One Cent"
8. "E Pluribus Unum"
9. Lincoln Memorial (12 columns)
10. Lincoln statue in middle of columns

<u>GENERAL</u>:
11. It is copper colored.
12. The rim around the edge on both sides is raised.
13. The front and back are inverted with respect to each other.
14. The diameter is 3/4 inch.
15. The thickness is approximately 1/16 inch.
16. Its weight is approximately 1/6 ounce.
17. The external rim is smooth on the outside.

THE HUMAN SPIDER WEB

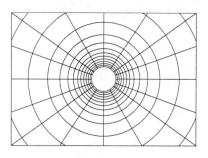

OBJECTIVES

✓ To provide an opportunity for members to work as a team
✓ To explore the dimensions of teamwork

MATERIALS

Adequate space in which to work

PROCEDURE

✓ Select (randomly) six to eight volunteers from the total group to participate in an exercise (for demonstration purposes). Have the group move to a location that allows them to stand in a small circle. Invite all other participants to position themselves where they can easily observe.

✓ Instruct each member of the small group to extend his or her left hand across the circle and grasp the left hand of another member who is approximately opposite. Then have them extend their right hands across the circle and grasp the right hands of other individuals.

✓ Inform them that their task is to unravel the spider web of interlocking arms *without letting go of anyone's hands.* They will also be timed (as a way to place pressure on them). The desired outcome is a circle of persons all holding the hands of the persons standing next to them.

DISCUSSION QUESTIONS

1. What was your first thought when you heard the nature of the task? (Probably, "This will be impossible!")
2. What member behaviors contributed to the success of your group?

3. What member behaviors detracted (or could detract) from its success in achieving its goal?

4. What lessons does this exercise have for future team building among our members?

TIPS

✓ Select only those wearing clothing that, when the wearers are bending or twisting to unravel themselves, either would not become soiled or would not result in personal embarrassment.

✓ If you are nervous about the success of this task, start with a smaller group (e.g., five persons), since the "web" will be simpler in that context.

✓ Some groups may be hesitant to start. If so, you might wish to provide one or two suggestions to initiate the action (e.g., "Tom, what if you were to step over the arms connecting Lionel and Raylene?")

✓ Bring a camera to record the action. The group members may relish seeing photographic evidence of their "before" and "after" positions!

IF YOU HAVE MORE TIME

✓ You may wish to divide a larger set of members into several smaller groups of six to eight persons, each of which will be competing with other groups to see who finishes the task first. Then have them explore what helped (and hindered) each group in the performance of its task.

✓ Alternatively, you might conduct the task, engage in a brief discussion to identify the important principles, and then ask the same group to repeat its task to see if they are now more capable of acting as a team.

EVERYONE HOLDS THE KEY TO THE PUZZLE

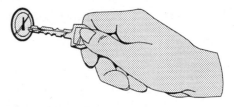

OBJECTIVE

To stress the importance of each team member's individual contributions and the importance of working together effectively as a group

MATERIALS

A picture puzzle, broken apart

PROCEDURE

✓ Before the session, select a solvable picture puzzle. Break it into subsets of five connectable pieces each.

✓ At the session, distribute a subset to each participant (such that the completed subsets can then be connected to each other).

✓ Instruct them to solve their own subset first, and then connect all the subsets appropriately until they have the total puzzle solved. Set a challenging time limit for the task completion, and possibly play some energizing music (e.g., the William Tell overture or Wagner's "Ride of the Valkyries") to create an additional sense of urgency.

DISCUSSION QUESTIONS

1. What reactions did you have when you realized your importance to the overall team?

2. What impact did the time deadline have on your effectiveness? What impact did the music have on your actions?

3. What was the impact of having team members available (and willing) to help you?

4. How did you feel when you had difficulty completing your subset of the puzzle? Did you feel comfortable asking for assistance?

TIPS

✓ You may choose to designate a small number of participants as free-floating "troubleshooters," who roam about the room and help those in trouble to see viable connections—both within their own subset and from one set to another.

✓ Depending on the number of group members and the difficulty level you choose (number of pieces allocated per person), you may not be able to use an entire puzzle. The key is to use only subsets of the master puzzle that are adjoining.

IF YOU HAVE MORE TIME

A key variable in this game is the degree of difficulty, which is a function of the time available for solving the overall puzzle and the number of pieces allocated to each participant. Therefore, you may wish to increase the number of pieces per person to about ten each.

MOST? BEST? GREATEST?

OBJECTIVES

✓ To encourage disclosure of personal information among group members

✓ To develop a norm of sharing

✓ To break down facades

✓ To increase awareness of each other's experiences

MATERIALS

None

PROCEDURE

✓ Select one provocative question for each meeting. You may choose either to announce it in advance (to give members time to think), or to introduce it on a spontaneous basis. To save time, ask each person to respond in 25 words or less.

✓ Then call on each person to give his or her self-report. Examples of good questions include:

- What is your greatest achievement?
- What was the happiest day of your life?
- What is your most prized possession?
- What is the most fun you ever had?
- What is your dream vacation like?
- What is the best book you have ever read?
- Who is your most admired person?
- If you could have a T-shirt printed with a message, what would it say?

The whole purpose is to encourage light-hearted self-disclosure (on a superficial level) that lends itself to future follow-up and probing in casual conversation.

DISCUSSION QUESTIONS

1. Is it acceptable to disclose personal thoughts, dreams, values, or achievements during work?

2. What are the positive consequences of doing so?

3. What possible concerns do you have about doing so as a result of this exercise?

4. What "norms" are we creating by this exercise? Why didn't they exist before?

TIPS

✓ Keep it moving quickly.

✓ You may wish to volunteer to be the first person to respond, to set the tone for the exercise.

✓ To protect individuals from any embarrassment, you may wish to create a "rule" that they can "pass" on a question once a month if they don't wish to answer.

IF YOU HAVE MORE TIME

Make the group responsible for generating future questions by passing the assignment for picking the next question around within the group. You might even wish to record a "living history" of member responses by saving a key word or two from each person, and distributing a follow-up handout listing member names and themes.

THE TIE THAT BINDS

OBJECTIVE

To demonstrate how closely tied to, and dependent on, several others each member is

MATERIALS

One very long piece (ball) of string

PROCEDURE

✓ Start by stressing the fact that we are all players in one or more *systems*. Systems thinking, according to popular writer/consultant Peter Senge, is a key ingredient in creating *learning organizations* (along with personal mastery, shared vision, and team learning).

✓ To illustrate your point, ask group members to think about who in the group they depend on for something.

✓ Point to one person, and give them a ball of string. Have them hold the loose end, and then—explaining one of their sources of support, data, counsel, or resources—throw the ball to that person. Continue the process until the group has exhausted their identifications of dependency.

DISCUSSION QUESTIONS

1. Even with the seemingly independent nature of our jobs, most of us still need others. How can you reconcile this apparent inconsistency?

2. How did you choose the person to whom you tossed the ball of string?

3. Who else could you have tossed the ball to?

4. Can you think of any cases where we operate totally without support from another?

5. In what ways do we acknowledge, or fail to give credit to, the persons that provide us with support?

6. Was anyone *not* identified as a source of aid?

TIPS

✓ You might want to do an informal assessment in advance, to assure yourself that no one would *not* be included in the strung-together system. If someone is likely not to be selected, simply start with them first.

✓ Have a camera handy to take a photograph of the final product. Make reprints and distribute them to the group at a subsequent meeting as a reminder of their "interconnectedness."

IF YOU HAVE MORE TIME

This game can also be played with pencil and paper. Prepare printed diagrams showing each member's name on the outer edge of a large circle. Have each member draw arrows on their chart showing whom they depend on. You can ask for two kinds of arrows: thick ones to show major dependency, and thin ones to show "other" kinds of dependency. The arrows should point from the aid giver to the recipient. Then produce a master diagram on chalkboard or flip chart that incorporates all the individual analyses. It will likely be an impressive web of interconnections!

GIVING AND GETTING

OBJECTIVE

To encourage participants to "reach out and help" other group members whenever necessary

MATERIALS

None

PROCEDURE

✓ Ask for a loan of one dollar from a member of the group. Displaying it prominently in one hand, proceed to ask for the loan of a second dollar from another member. Then carefully repay the first loaner with the second dollar, and repay the second loaner with the first dollar. Then ask the rhetorical question, "Is either of these persons now richer than they were before the exchange?" (Neither is, of course.)

✓ Then point out to the group that, by contrast, had two *ideas* been shared as readily, their respective givers would be richer in experience than they were before. In addition, of course, even the rest of us (bystanders) might be richer.

DISCUSSION QUESTIONS

1. What factors seem to *prevent* us from sharing useful ideas and insights with other group members?

2. What factors should *encourage* us to share ideas and advice with others on a regular basis?

3. What are the underlying behavioral reasons *why* we should aid others (e.g., the law of reciprocity, mutual dependency/ expected mutual benefit)?

TIP

It is wise to pick a generic problem for the group to focus on. Then, when ideas are generated, almost everyone can gain from them and be "richer."

IF YOU HAVE MORE TIME

Give each participant one or more pieces of pre-printed play money (with a blank back side). Let them exchange the money with each other first to experience the lack of enrichment that ensues. Then ask each person to write at least one idea on the play money and give it to the appropriate person.

A BAG FULL OF MONEY

OBJECTIVE

To allow the group to do "blue-sky" think-ing without fiscal restraints

MATERIALS

Paper, pens or pencils

PROCEDURE

✓ Tell the group that some unknown philanthropist has just dropped off a bag full of money for you to spend for your firm or organization. The bag contains $500,000 with the note that there are absolutely no constraints, except that the money must be spent strictly on items for the organization. In other words, there can be no vacation trips to Hawaii or other types of personal indulgences.

✓ Form groups of three and have the group write out their "wish list" for the organization, and figure out a fair approximation of the costs involved.

✓ After sufficient time is allowed, have each group report their results.

DISCUSSION QUESTIONS

1. How many of you changed your individual thoughts after con-sulting with your team?

2. Was the group's response better than the individuals'? Why?

3. Although groups may often produce better decisions, are there not some cautions as well?

4. If your top priority is really an important one, what are some ways we might convince those in charge of that necessity?

✓ Advise the group that, even though the money can't be used for personal expenditures, they may use their creativity in identifying items that would bring some return on investment.

✓ If a group suggests they'd like to take the team to spend a day with a well-known guru in their field, allow that as perfectly acceptable, but tell them to include costs of airfares, lodgings, and other related items.

TEAM LEADERSHIP TEST

OBJECTIVES

✓ To give leaders and managers an opportunity for self-assessment
✓ To show areas that might be improved

MATERIALS

Copies of the Leadership Pre-/Posttest

PROCEDURE

✓ Review the Leadership Pre-/Posttest and make any additions, corrections, or changes as appropriate for your organization.
✓ Distribute copies to your group and ask that they individually assess themselves on the items shown. Do not collect the completed forms, but suggest that they hold on to them for a few weeks.
✓ After that interval, ask them to review their own ratings and then note in which areas they believe they have shown improvement and which areas might still need some attention.

DISCUSSION QUESTIONS

1. Which items seem to be the most important in your job today?
2. Would you have answered question 1 differently last year at this time?
3. How have you acquired the knowledge and skills to this point in your career?
4. What should (could) be done to assist you in improving the areas you feel need to be addressed?

TIP

The questions posed are applicable to most any organization. For internal use, change, add, or alter the items to better fit the particular group and work assignment.

LEADERSHIP PRE-/POSTTEST

Name _____

Assess your leadership skills on a scale from 1 to 10 (where 1 = low and 10 = very high). Mark an X on the number below each statement.

_____ **1.** How much do you know about how to motivate people?
      1   2   3   4   5   6   7   8   9   10

_____ **2.** How good are you at talking to groups and communicating?
      1   2   3   4   5   6   7   8   9   10

_____ **3.** How do you think others would rate you as a leader?
      1   2   3   4   5   6   7   8   9   10

_____ **4.** How would you rate yourself as a leader?
      1   2   3   4   5   6   7   8   9   10

_____ **5.** How good are you at dealing with difficult people?
      1   2   3   4   5   6   7   8   9   10

_____ **6.** How likely are you to introduce yourself to people you don't know?
      1   2   3   4   5   6   7   8   9   10

_____ **7.** How much do you know about leadership?
      1   2   3   4   5   6   7   8   9   10

_____ **8.** How much leadership experience do you have?
      1   2   3   4   5   6   7   8   9   10

_____ **9.** How well do you work under pressure?
      1   2   3   4   5   6   7   8   9   10

_____ **10.** How important are you to the overall success of your organization?
      1   2   3   4   5   6   7   8   9   10

_____ **TOTAL SCORE** (Add your answers and mark the total.)

Now read the questions again and check, in the left-hand column, the three topics that you would like to learn more about.

TRAITS OF LEADERSHIP

OBJECTIVE

To illustrate the traits and qualities that are imperative for success in dealing with today's diverse workforce

MATERIALS

Paper, pens or pencils

PROCEDURE

✓ In discussing the areas of leadership, management, or working with teams in a diverse workplace setting, it is apparent that the skills of a manager ten years ago compared with those of the leader today are quite different.

✓ Ask the group to individually think of five or six people that they consider real "leaders" today. These names could come from business, government, religion, education, or any other area.

✓ Give them a few minutes to think about and jot down their list, and ask that they also add a note as to why each of the names came to mind.

✓ Then form groups of three or four people, and ask them to compare and contrast their lists, and, more importantly, why these names surfaced.

DISCUSSION QUESTIONS

1. What are some of the names most of you had in common?
2. Why did these names come up so often?
3. Who has a name that many of us perhaps wouldn't know (a former teacher, parent, sibling, coach)? Tell us why?
4. How do you think your list might differ if we did this five or even ten years ago?

✓ To start the discussion, you might throw out a few names that will start their thinking.

✓ Also, suggest that the names can be past or present leaders, such as Walt Disney, Abraham Lincoln, among others.

7

Presentation Boosters

RAPID REVIEW

OBJECTIVE

To provide a method for quick review and summary of the important insights gained and conclusions reached

MATERIALS

None, other than a chalkboard or flip chart for recording responses

PROCEDURE

✓ After a presentation, and just prior to a scheduled break, remind the participants that the discussion has ranged far and wide across topics. To check on what they've heard so far, you're going to do a quick review. Before you break the session, invite them to summarize *the key things they've learned or concluded to this point.*

✓ Then, as rapidly as possible, ask for responses. After each one, say "Thank you, that's one" and so on, until ten (or more) key points are stated.

DISCUSSION QUESTIONS

1. How many were surprised by the nature of items the group generated?
2. What is the value in learning what others considered to be the most important items?
3. In what ways was your private list different from that of others?

TIP

The number of points that you solicit from the group is arbitrarily chosen each time by the group leader. It could be as few as three, or unlimited (until the ideas run out). The number will depend on the time available, as well as on the diversity of the discussion topics.

IF YOU HAVE MORE TIME

Ask the group members to brainstorm their own lists first. Then ask the group to generate a master list. This provides a rich opportunity for individuals to compare their own perspectives and assessments of importance to those of their colleagues.

WHAT'S ON YOUR MIND?

OBJECTIVE

To alert group members to the need to focus 100% of their energies on the agenda for today, setting aside all other concerns and distractions

MATERIALS

One 3 × 5 card for each group member, and pens or pencils

PROCEDURE

✓ Distribute a card to each person. Ask them to write down the key issues, problems, or dilemmas that are currently on their mind.
✓ Direct them to place the card in their pocket or purse and not refer to it for the remainder of the meeting.
✓ Then introduce the major agenda item for the day.
✓ At the end of the meeting, give members of the group "permission" to refocus on their personal problems and issues.

DISCUSSION QUESTION

After the session, ask group members how effective the technique was. Suggest that it is difficult to hold two competing thoughts in our minds at the same time, and that we all need to practice the ability to focus our efforts and shut out unrelated distractions.

TIP

For a group that is slow to "buy into" a game of this type, you might want to stimulate their thoughts by sharing examples of the types of distractions that might be in someone's mind, such as:

- Buying an anniversary present for my spouse.
- Calling the airlines for reservations.
- Finishing up project XYZ.

IF YOU HAVE MORE TIME

You can be more dramatic with the game by giving each person an envelope and asking them to symbolically "put away their problems" by placing the card into the envelope, sealing it, and identifying it as theirs. You then collect the envelopes for the duration of the meeting. Then, when the meeting is over, distribute the envelopes to each person again.

POKER-FACED PARTICIPATION

OBJECTIVE

To stimulate a higher level, and a broader distribution, of member participation in the group's discussions

MATERIALS

A deck of playing cards

PROCEDURE

Some people are reluctant to get involved in open discussions, especially if they are new members, face a complex or threatening issue, or don't feel comfortable with the leader yet. You can break the ice quickly and stimulate broader (even competitive) group participation in response to your questions by following this method:

✓ Inform the group that they will have the opportunity to play one hand of poker at the end of the meeting. The person with the best overall poker hand will win a prize.

✓ Give one card to each person every time they make a meaningful contribution to the discussion.

✓ At the end of the session, clarify the winning order of poker hands (i.e., royal flush, straight flush, four of a kind, full house, flush, straight, three of a kind, two pair, one pair). Then identify the best five-card hand in the group and award a prize.

DISCUSSION QUESTIONS

1. What impact did this technique have on your *participation*?
2. What carry-over impact will it have on your participation in *subsequent* meetings?
3. Did this aid or interfere with your *learning* about the day's discussion topic?

TIPS

✓ *Liberally* reward participants with randomly drawn cards as they engage in discussion. The purpose at this stage is less to judge the quality of ideas than to encourage comfortable participation.

✓ If you deem poker an unacceptable structure for this exercise, simply award the prize to the person with the highest point total (with all face cards counting as 10).

IF YOU HAVE MORE TIME

This game also works well with small groups. Form teams of three to five persons in advance, and award cards as before. Then give the teams two minutes at the end of discussion to pool their resources and form the best poker hand that they can. Be sure to have a prize that the *team* can share (e.g., a six pack of soda)!

FAIRNESS IN NEGOTIATIONS

OBJECTIVE

To stress the importance of perceptions of equity and fairness in any contact or negotiation

MATERIALS

A substantial supply of a tangible item that is likely to be mutually desirable by two persons present

PROCEDURE

✓ Identify two people to role play an interaction. Designate them A and B.

✓ Visibly provide Individual A with a supply of goods to distribute to (share with) B. This may be $100 in (play) money, 100 jelly beans, or M&Ms. Instruct A that he or she is to make an offer to split the resource with B in any proportion desired. B may only accept or reject the offer, but not negotiate the split. If B accepts the offer, a deal is made. If B rejects the offer, neither party is to receive any of the items.

✓ Inform B that A has 100 of the resource items to be shared between them. B can accept or reject the single offer to be made, but may not provide any input into A's determination of the offer, nor may a counteroffer be made. If B rejects the offer, neither party keeps any of the items.

✓ Proceed with the role play interaction.

DISCUSSION QUESTIONS

1. Why did A behave as he or she did?

2. Why did B respond as he or she did?

3. What advice do you have for people like A and B in these situations at work?

A often is tempted to offer a split that will be personally favorable, such as 60-40 or 80-20. This reflects a world in which individuals compete for resources and are taught to "win" at all costs. From a rational perspective, B should accept *any* offer from A since B will be better off with *anything* (even 1) than previously. But since people don't like to be exploited, many B's will reject offers that don't seem *fair* (as perceived by them). Similarly, A could decide to offer *any* split (even 1-99), since that would make A better off than before. Apparently, the key to making a deal of this kind is not only to convince the other party that they will gain a lot, but also to create an image of *fairness*, wherein B is convinced that A won't be gaining a lot more than B. Even when it is possible to "make a killing" on a single deal, it may be wiser to build a longer-term relationship by offering a *fair* deal. This requires, of course, either empathizing sufficiently to infer what is fair, or inquiring of the other party what would be a fair resolution to the situation.

IF YOU HAVE MORE TIME

✓ After the first role play, ask for new volunteers before discussing the incident, and then repeat the process.

✓ Repeat the process, allowing B to make a single counteroffer to A.

HOW DID THIS MEETING GO?

OBJECTIVE

To encourage honest feedback from group members at the conclusion of a meeting or discussion

MATERIALS

Two flip charts and several colored markers

PROCEDURE

✓ Place two flip charts at the front of the room.

- On the first, write: "Here are some things we especially valued about the way the meeting was run today."

- On the second flip chart, write: "Here are some suggestions as to how future meetings like this could be even better ..."

✓ Invite participants to spend the next six to eight minutes "processing" the meeting (consciously reflecting on it and examining both what went well and what merits improvement). Record the essence of all ideas.

✓ Thank them for their suggestions and comments.

✓ Tear off the flip charts and return to your office. You may choose to type up the comments and distribute them to the group members, or you may simply study them yourself to identify any relevant themes or constructive comments affecting things within your control. Then celebrate your success, and change something needing improvement!

DISCUSSION QUESTIONS

1. Which items is there agreement on?

2. Which items is there disagreement on? How can that disagreement be resolved to the relative satisfaction of all concerned?

3. What actions can individual members commit to engaging in to improve meeting effectiveness?

If the trust level between you and the group is not yet very high, you may want to try a more anonymous procedure the first time or two. After posting the two questions on the wall for the group, tell participants that you will be leaving the room for the next ten minutes and you sincerely ask their honest evaluation of the meeting. Ask them to write down their individual responses to the two questions posed. Explain that they should not sign their names, but you would appreciate their specific suggestions and assessment. If participants are still writing their comments after ten minutes, allow a few more minutes. When you return, express your appreciation to them and take the flip charts back to your work site for careful analysis (don't be defensive!). Then be sure to follow up with meaningful changes in subsequent meetings!

IF YOU HAVE MORE TIME

After identifying what went well and what needs improvement, ask the group to convert those comments into specific, *action-oriented implications.* What new behaviors would they recommend for both you and themselves that would improve the effectiveness of future meetings?

8

Communication, Listening, and Feedback Activities

LET'S PLAY BALL!

OBJECTIVE

To emphasize the importance of engaging in active listening during a discussion

MATERIALS

One soft (e.g., Nerf) ball

PROCEDURE

✓ Take out a soft, catchable ball. Select one group member and offer to play catch with that person for awhile. Throw the ball back and forth for a minute or two.

✓ After the pattern has been firmly established, invite the other team members to participate. Make sure that no one is neglected; if so, direct the ball to that individual. If the ball comes to you too frequently, discourage this by either continually dropping it or even turning your back so as to avoid becoming a target.

✓ Lead the group in a brief discussion of what just took place.

DISCUSSION QUESTIONS

1. How did you feel when only one person and I were playing catch?

2. Did you observe more spontaneity, smiles, and overall involvement when the entire group was participating? Why?

3. What are the lessons here for our team (e.g., that we can all learn from each other *if* we all agree to become actively involved in both the listening and contributing process)?

4. What group skills are necessary for widespread participation in our team?

154

TIP

Make sure that the group "catches" several points from this exercise—wide participation is needed, passive members are not as valuable, good listening skills are needed, all must be watchful.

IF YOU HAVE MORE TIME

Have the group explore the reasons why some people do not choose to participate as actively. Have the group generate a list of ways to enhance their demonstration of active listening skills.

CAN WE TALK?

OBJECTIVE

To stress the importance of perceptions, and to encourage group members to check each other's key perceptions regularly

MATERIALS

Copies of the "Research Report on the Extent of Typical Superior–Subordinate Misunderstanding" handout

PROCEDURE

✓ Ask the group members to list the major areas of their job responsibilities (e.g., the ten most important tasks).

✓ Ask them to predict how many of those ten tasks or areas their manager would list if she or he were asked to do so.

✓ Distribute copies of the handout, showing that there is a "typical" 25% lack of overlap between superior–subordinate perceptions.

DISCUSSION QUESTIONS

1. If there is a difference between what you reported in the first two steps in the procedure, why do you think this exists?

2. What do you think the typical disparity is throughout the unit?

3. What specific action steps could (will) you take to resolve this problem?

TIP

Some individuals may be reluctant to engage in such an exercise, in which either party is fearful of embarrassment because of forgetting or overlooking a key dimension of their (or the other's) job. It is best to set a relaxed tone for this "game," by indicating that the surprise element and lack of preparation time are likely contributors to the mismatched lists.

✓ The ideal approach is to have superior–subordinate pairs prepare independent lists in advance of the session. Then they can get together to compare their lists and have "real" data about perceptual differences. If this is not possible, then encourage each of them to contact their manager following the meeting to explore his or her perceptions.

✓ A modification or extension of this exercise is to ask the group to assess (1) the personal qualifications needed to perform their jobs; (2) the job changes that will be forthcoming; or (3) the current obstacles to effective performance. Many of these estimates will be even higher than 25%.

RESEARCH REPORTS ON THE EXTENT OF TYPICAL SUPERIOR-SUBORDINATE MISUNDERSTANDING

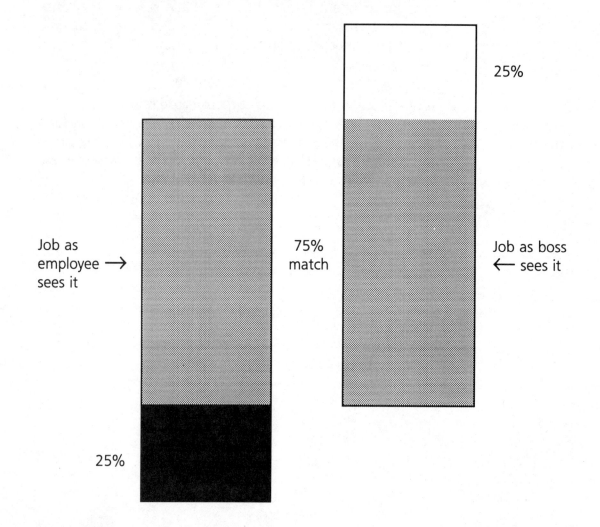

Job as employee → sees it

75% match

Job as boss ← sees it

25%

25%

Key:

■ What the employee is paying attention to that the boss does not perceive to be important.

□ What the boss expects the employee to pay attention to, but the employee does not perceive as important.

▒ Areas of agreement between boss and subordinate.

FIRE, AIM, READY?

OBJECTIVE

To demonstrate that people don't always read (or follow) even simple directions

MATERIALS

Enough copies of the Arithmetic Test for all members

PROCEDURE

✓ Pass out copies of the test—*face down.*

✓ Indicate that you will be asking them to solve some very simple problems in arithmetic, involving addition, subtraction, multiplication, and division.

✓ State, "As soon as I say 'Go,' turn your papers over, read over the entire exercise, and follow the directions. Work as fast as you can, as there is a prize available to the first one to finish (and do so accurately) within 60 seconds."

✓ Say, "Go!"

✓ Immediately start to count down the seconds remaining (i.e., 59, 58, 57, ...) just loudly enough for all members to hear.

✓ When time is up, quickly ask them to report the answers obtained to each question (e.g., "The answer to question 1 is what?" "Question 2?"). Members will soon discover that some of them have different answers. You might facetiously ask them, "Did you all get the same sheet?" Then let the group discover their problem by reading the directions to themselves.

DISCUSSION QUESTIONS

1. Remember the old saying, "If all else fails, read the directions!"? Why didn't we do so here?

    a. We were pressed for time.

    b. We didn't think it was necessary.

    c. We saw what looked like "familiar" problems.

    d. Directions are often a waste of time.

2. Have you ever seen incidents where poorly given or rushed instructions may be worse than none at all?

3. Did you experience pressure at the start of this exercise? What effects did this have on your performance?

4. In what ways did we fall prey to the trap of "Fire, aim, ready"? In other words, are we sometimes *too* quick to act before we analyze and prepare?

5. What lessons does this exercise have for us?

TIPS

✓ Make certain that your final instructions are given hurriedly and allow no time for questions.

✓ Be careful not to embarass anyone for their error. The point is to demonstrate an all-too-common tendency, not a specific person's behavioral problem.

ARITHMETIC TEST

Directions: In the following simple arithmetic problems, a plus (+) sign means to multiply, a divide (÷) sign means to add, a minus (−) sign means to divide, and a times (×) sign means to subtract. Complete the problems following these directions.

8 +2 = _____	14 − 7 = _____
9 + 11 = _____	6 × 5 = _____
4 × 3 = _____	8 + 3 = _____
6 ÷ 2 = _____	7 × 2 = _____
9 − 3 = _____	9 + 2 = _____
7 × 4 = _____	8 − 4 = _____
4 + 4 = _____	9 + 6 = _____
8 − 4 = _____	1 ÷ 1 = _____
12 × 2 = _____	8 × 7 = _____
20 − 10 = _____	13 − 1 = _____
9 − 1 = _____	16 − 4 = _____
5 + 6 = _____	8 × 2 = _____
2 × 1 = _____	9 ÷ 9 = _____
10 − 5 = _____	6 × 2 = _____
12 + 2 = _____	8 + 4 = _____
6 ÷ 6 = _____	10 − 2 = _____
8 + 5 = _____	4 − 1 = _____
6 + 6 = _____	18 − 3 = _____
17 × 2 = _____	8 + 2 = _____
14 ÷ 7 = _____	15 × 3 = _____

NONVERBAL INTRODUCTIONS

OBJECTIVE

To demonstrate that nonverbal communications or body language can often be very effective in "communicating" with others

MATERIALS

None

PROCEDURE

✓ Divide participants into groups of two and state that the purpose of this exercise is to illustrate the importance of nonverbal communication.

✓ At your signal, one person will "introduce" him-/herself to the other individual. They can use any prop, visual, pictures, signs, gestures, etc. they wish. However, they may not talk!

✓ At the end of two minutes, call time and then ask the second person to do the same thing, i.e., no talking.

✓ After an additional two minutes, call for the group's attention, and ask each person to discuss with their partner their "reading" of the other's body language.

DISCUSSION QUESTIONS

1. How accurate were you in interpreting your partner's body language?

2. What were some of the more creative ways you devised to make your point?

3. Was it difficult for some of us to describe ourselves without using words?

4. What barriers seemed to get in the way of nonverbal communication?

5. In what ways might these barriers be lessened?

TIPS

✓ As you are forming the two-person teams, try to get people together who preferably are not acquainted or who at least don't know one another well.

✓ Make it a fun exercise. Before you call time after the first person introduces him-/herself, comment about some of the more creative gestures and signals you see.

LET'S TALK

OBJECTIVE

To illustrate how quickly people can get to know others in an informal setting

MATERIALS

None

PROCEDURE

✓ Advise the group that, even though we all work together, we often know our colleagues on a superficial basis, and never really get a chance to learn more about others.

✓ Ask each person to find a partner—preferable one they don't know very well.

✓ Then tell them they will have two to three minutes to talk to each other. That's it—let's talk. They can talk about anything they want—even the weather—but preferably they should tell each other some things about themselves.

DISCUSSION QUESTIONS

1. How well do you feel you "know" your new friend?
2. Did two or three minutes seem to go very quickly?
3. Do any of us feel we now know our new friends better than we know old friends?
4. Why don't we always take the time to do this with other co-workers?

TIPS

✓ To make the activity more user-friendly, suggest to the group that it's really OK to talk about yourselves, i.e., your background, home town, schooling, and so on.

✓ Initially, some individuals may find it awkward or difficult to "just talk." Encourage them to open up to their partners. They can discuss hobbies, previous jobs, or anything about themselves.

✓ Midway through the time frame, ask the group to ensure that each person has some time to talk. If only one person has spoken so far, have the other talk now.

THE ANIMAL ANALOGY

OBJECTIVE

To allow leaders, managers, and others to get a pulse or picture of their leadership style from others in a light, nonthreatening manner

MATERIALS

None

PROCEDURE

At the conclusion of a staff meeting or other organizational get-together, inform the group that you would be interested in some type of feedback on the way you conducted the meeting. Rather than verbal or written evaluation, ask each person to sketch out a picture of whatever animal they can think of to depict the way you led the session. Make sure they understand that they must keep it light!

DISCUSSION QUESTIONS

1. How did you react when we asked for your honest opinions in this task?

2. What are some other ways we could have gotten this feedback?

3. If some of your co-workers see their own managers as bullish individuals, how might they tactfully tell their bosses?

4. What might be considered the "ideal" animal in this case? Why?

TIPS

✓ If you describe yourself as a task-master, humorously inform the group that a previous group gave you three bulls and two elephants!

✓ Continue to keep this a fun activity. Let the group know that you're interested in their reactions, but "be nice to me." In other words, this is not the place for ax-grinding or other kinds of negativity.

✓ *Caution:* Don't use this activity when the meeting itself addressed items of a controversial or sensitive nature.

About the author

Dr. John W. Newstrom is a university professor, noted author, and consultant to organizations in the areas of training and supervisory development. He is currently a Professor of Human Resource Management in the School of Business and Economics at the University of Minnesota, Duluth, where he teaches courses and workshops in the fields of Organizational Change, Human Resource Development, Management, and Interpersonal and Group Relations. He has conducted training programs on a wide range of topics for organizations including 3M Co., Lakehead Pipeline, LTV Steel Mining, Blandin Paper Co., Diamond Tool, Minnesota Power, Clyde Iron, City of Scottsdale, Armour-Dial, and St. Luke's Hospital.

John has been active in the American Society for Training and Development (ASTD) since 1971, holding elective offices in the Valley of the Sun (Phoenix) and Lake Superior (Duluth) chapters. His involvement with national ASTD includes a dozen presentations to national conferences, service on the National Board of Directors, Budget and Finance Committee, and as the lead instructor for the Basics of Training workshop, which he taught nationally for ASTD for seven years. He was the recipient of a Special Recognition Award for Outstanding Support to Region VI, ASTD in 1992. He has been a popular speaker, appearing before many ASTD chapters throughout the United States.

Dr. Newstrom has written ten articles for the *Training and Development Journal* on topics such as needs analysis, evaluation, transfer of training, andragogy, and unlearning; he serves on the Editorial Review Board for the *Journal of Management Development,* and as a reviewer for the *Human Resource Development Quarterly;* and he is the co-author (with Ed Scannell) of the widely acclaimed books *Games Trainers Play, More Games Trainers Play, Still More Games Trainers Play,* and *Even More Games Trainers Play.* He has also co-authored, in recent years:

- *The Manager's Bookshelf* (with Jon Pierce)
- *Organizational Behavior* (with Keith Davis)
- *Windows into Organizations* (with Jon Pierce)
- *What Every Supervisor Should Know* (with Lester Bittel)
- *Transfer of Training* (with Mary Broad)
- *Leaders and the Leadership Process* (with Jon Pierce)

A member of the National Speakers Association (NSA), **Edward E. Scannell** has given more than a thousand presentations, seminars, and workshops across the United States and internationally. He was the 1985 recipient of the President's Award from the NSA, and served as the 1987–88 President of the Arizona chapter. He received his C.S.P. (Certified Speaking Professional) designation in 1986. He has served on NSA's Board of Directors, and was the National President for NSA in 1991–92.

Ed has written or coauthored nine books and over fifty articles in the fields of human resource development, communication, creativity, meeting planning, and management. His *Games Trainers Play* series of books (written with John W. Newstrom) is used by speakers, trainers, facilitators, consultants, and meeting planners all around the world.

Actively involved in both civic and professional organizations, he has served on the Boards of Directors of a number of groups including the Tempe Chamber of Commerce, the American Society for Training and Development (ASTD), the National Speakers Association, and Meeting Planners International (MPI). He was the 1982 National President of ASTD and a recipient of its prestigious Gordon M. Bliss award. He later served a two-year term as the Executive Chairman of the Board of the International Federation of Training and Development Organizations. Ed is a Past President of MPI Arizona's Sunbelt Chapter, and its 1986 Planner of the Year. He was elected MPI International President in 1988–89. He has since served as a trustee for the MPI Educational Research Foundation.

Ed was the Director of the University Conference Bureau at Arizona State University for several years. Prior to that position, he taught at the ASU College of Business and at the University of Northern Iowa. As recognition of his activities, he is listed in:

- *Leaders in Education*
- *Personalities of the West and Midwest*
- *Who's Who in the West*
- *Dictionary of International Biography*
- *Men of Achievement*